Fundamentals of Physical Design and Query Compilation

Synthesis Lectures on Data Management

Editor
M. Tamer Özsu, *University of Waterloo*

Synthesis Lectures on Data Management is edited by Tamer Özsu of the University of Waterloo. The series will publish 50- to 125 page publications on topics pertaining to data management. The scope will largely follow the purview of premier information and computer science conferences, such as ACM SIGMOD, VLDB, ICDE, PODS, ICDT, and ACM KDD. Potential topics include, but not are limited to: query languages, database system architectures, transaction management, data warehousing, XML and databases, data stream systems, wide scale data distribution, multimedia data

Fundamentals of Physical Design and Query Compilation

David Toman and Grant Weddell

ISBN:978-3-031-00753-8   paperback
ISBN: 978-3-031-01881-7   ebook

DOI 10.1007/978-3-031-01881-7

A Publication in the Springer series
SYNTHESIS LECTURES ON DATA MANAGEMENT

Lecture #18
Series Editor: M. Tamer Özsu, *University of Waterloo*
Series ISSN
Synthesis Lectures on Data Management
Print 2153-5418   Electronic 2153-5426

Fundamentals of Physical Design and Query Compilation

David Toman and Grant Weddell
University of Waterloo, Canada

SYNTHESIS LECTURES ON DATA MANAGEMENT #18

ABSTRACT

Query compilation is the problem of translating user requests formulated over purely conceptual and domain specific ways of understanding data, commonly called logical designs, to efficient executable programs called query plans. Such plans access various concrete data sources through their low-level often iterator-based interfaces. An appreciation of the concrete data sources, their interfaces and how such capabilities relate to logical design is commonly called a physical design. This book is an introduction to the fundamental methods underlying database technology that solves the problem of query compilation. The methods are presented in terms of first-order logic which serves as the vehicle for specifying physical design, expressing user requests and query plans, and understanding how query plans implement user requests.

KEYWORDS

query compilation, semantic query optimization, physical database design, database update, logical foundations and integrity constraints, bag semantics and query plans

Contents

Preface

Information abounds, and the arrival of commercially viable computer systems with mass storage to help manage information has prompted the development of database systems together with an underlying technology. This book is about an important part of the technology for database systems that require only a logical appreciation of data on the part of application developers, such as database systems that support the relational model of data: the part that enables users to formulate queries that are devoid of any information relating to concrete data sources and their low-level interfaces.

A fundamental problem that must therefore be addressed is to translate user requests over purely conceptual and domain-specific ways of understanding of data, commonly called *logical designs*, to efficient executable programs, called *query plans*, for evaluating the requests by accessing various concrete data sources through their low-level often iterator-based interfaces. An appreciation of the concrete data sources, their interfaces and how such capabilities relate to logical design is in turn called a *physical design*. There are several phrases used to refer to the problem of translating user requests to plans; *plan generation* and *query optimization* are examples. In this book, we use *query compilation* to emphasize our focus on the issue of determining when plans correctly implement user requests.

The lingua franca throughout the book is *first-order logic* (FOL). Indeed, we shall see that FOL suffices to satisfy a number of needs connected with capturing and reasoning about physical design and query compilation.

1. It is a convenient language in which to formulate logical designs.

2. User queries correspond naturally to well-formed formulae in FOL. In fact, a subset of well-formed formulae that satisfy a condition called *domain independence* constitute a standard metric of query expressiveness called *relational completeness*.

3. With the added notion of *binding patterns*, it is also a convenient language to capture physical designs. This remains true for very sophisticated designs that entail multi-level store, pointers, hashing, capabilities for runtime typing, user defined functions, and so on.

4. Additional syntactic conditions on well-formed formulae in FOL lead to a plan language with a small set of primitive operations that suffice to formulate query plans over sophisticated physical designs that are often "built-in" in existing relational database technology.

5. Query compilation, the problem of synthesizing plans for user queries, corresponds naturally to reasoning in FOL. In the book, we look at how both chase-based reasoning and more general reasoning based on interpolation in FOL can be used to synthesize plans for user queries that express both requests for information and for data update.

The book is organized into six chapters. A more thorough introduction to basic terminology and notation for the problems of physical design and query compilation are the subject of Chapter 1. Items 1–4 above are the subject of the next three chapters. In particular, Chapters 2 and 3 review how FOL in combination with binding patterns can be used to formally capture both logical and physical design, to express user queries, and, with some straightforward extensions relating to syntax, to express query plans that implement user queries by appealing to a small set of primitive operations. Chapter 4 presents a number of cases that demonstrate how such a minimalist approach can be coupled with constraints expressed in FOL in ways that manifest sophisticated data structures and algorithms that are often implemented as additional native data encoding options and query operations in existing relational database technology. (Some examples are listed in Item 3 above.) The last item is the subject of the remaining two chapters. In particular, approaches to the problem of query compilation are considered in Chapter 5 and applications of these techniques to the problem of database update in Chapter 6.

A brief overview of FOL is given in Appendix A for readers who might require a review of basic material. It is a good idea to read through Appendix A to at least align expectations of FOL terminology and notation with what is presumed in this book. The book also presumes that readers are familiar with the subject of computer science to the extent that is acquired during the first two years of an undergraduate degree. This includes an understanding of algorithms and data structures, basic computational and complexity issues and imperative programming. An introductory course on mathematical logic and on databases is also desirable, in particular on declarative programming in SQL.

Following each chapter is a brief bibliography relevant to the topic and a list of exercises on topics that can be used as the basis for a class discussion. Many are sufficiently general that they can also be used as the basis for a term project.

David Toman and Grant Weddell
July 2011

Acknowledgments

The authors would like to thank the National Institute of Informatics (NII, Tokyo) for providing the opportunity to deliver a lecture series based on an earlier version of the material discussed in this book. We would also like to express our thanks to Tamer Özsu for his support and encouragement throughout.

David Toman and Grant Weddell
July 2011

CHAPTER 1

Introduction

The goals for this chapter are to introduce basic terminology and notation for the fundamental problems of physical design and query compilation in database systems that require only a logical appreciation of data on the part of application developers, such as database systems that support the relational model of data. This shields developers from any need to appreciate how data is encoded by low level concrete data structures or by legacy data sources. We do this by appealing to an example scenario for a hypothetical enterprise called ACME Corporation. Our scenario assumes that ACME, like all enterprises, needs to carefully manage information about its personnel, their salaries, and so on.

1.1 LOGICAL AND PHYSICAL DESIGN

There is a rough dichotomy of information in database systems into what are commonly termed *data* and *metadata*. For example, data important to ACME's management of its personnel might include the following information.

1. Mary is an employee.

2. Mary's employee number is 3412.

3. Mary's salary is 72000.

Accordingly, the following metadata might also be important to ACME.

4. There is a kind of entity called an `employee`.

5. There are attributes called `employee-number`, `name` and `salary`.

6. Each employee entity has attributes `employee-number`, `name` and `salary`.

7. Employees are identified by their `employee-number`.

Now assume the need to manage such information has prompted ACME to develop a computer-based information system *using relational database technology* called PAYROLL. The infrastructure for PAYROLL consists of a computer system with mass storage and two separate departments called APS and DBA. APS is short for *applications* and is responsible for PAYROLL itself, whereas DBA is short for *database administration* and is responsible for managing the computer system resource.

To be productive, personnel in DBA must understand how the computer system can best be used to support the daily *workload* on PAYROLL. A workload refers to the pattern and frequency of *queries* that encode search and update requests on PAYROLL data. In particular, personnel in DBA have the responsibility for choosing file formats and data structures to *physically encode* PAYROLL data on mass storage in a way that makes the best use of the computer system. This in turn requires some appreciation of the above PAYROLL metadata, of the volume of PAYROLL data and of typical workloads. In short, part of the mandate for DBA includes responsibility for the *physical design* of PAYROLL.

For ACME's PAYROLL system, metadata that reflects a physical design choice by DBA might include the following additional information.

8. There is a file of records called `emp-file`.

9. There are record fields `emp-num`, `emp-name` and `emp-salary`.

10. Each `emp-file` record has the fields `emp-num`, `emp-name` and `emp-salary`.

11. File `emp-file` is organized as a B-tree data structure that supports an `emp-lookup` operation, given a value for attribute `employee-number`.

12. Records in file `emp-file` correspond one-to-one with `employee` entities.

13. Record fields in file `emp-file` encode the corresponding attribute values for `employee` entities, for example, `emp-num` encodes an `employee-number`.

In contrast, for personnel in APS to be productive, they will need to have a thorough understanding of 4 through 7 above. They must become familiar with the concept of an `employee`, of a `salary`, of how an unambiguous reference to an employee is accomplished with an `employee-number`, and so on. In short, part of the mandate for APS includes responsibility for the *logical design* of PAYROLL, a design that effectively distills a *conceptual* appreciation of PAYROLL information needed by ACME. However, since PAYROLL uses relational database technology, there is no need for personnel in APS to also become familiar with the physical design of PAYROLL. Most importantly, this will mean that all PAYROLL code written by APS personnel that encodes queries on PAYROLL data will be devoid of any mention of file names such as `emp-file` or interfaces to data structures such as `emp-lookup`. In such a circumstance, queries are said to be *physically data independent*.

Thus, a fundamental task for a relational database system is to *compile* queries that are physically data independent to concrete *query plans* that are expressed in terms of operations defined by a given physical design, that is, by operations provided by the various data structures, files, records and record fields that encode relevant data. For example, code for PAYROLL written by personnel in APS might include the following parameterized query.

14. Find the `salary` for any `employee` whose `employee-number` is given by a parameter p.

Since the query has no reference to any vocabulary relating to physical design, the query is physically data independent.

By virtue of DBA's decisions on a choice of physical database design for PAYROLL, the database system might compile this request to the following query plan.

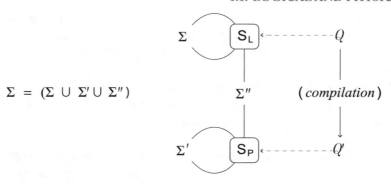

$$\Sigma = (\Sigma \cup \Sigma' \cup \Sigma'')$$

Figure 1.1: On physical design and query compilation.

15. Invoke operation `emp-lookup(p)`, just once, on file `emp-file`. If an `emp-file` record is found, then extract and return the value of field `emp-salary`.

Since this alternative formulation of the query mentions vocabulary specific to physical design, such as `emp-file` and `emp-salary`, the query is no longer physically data independent. In fact, this formulation is sufficiently concrete that it is now *executable*.

It is this underlying problem of *query compilation* that is the subject of this book. An overall view of the problem is given in Figure 1.1 in which we introduce a number of symbols that will be used in the remaining chapters. We return to our example scenario of ACME's PAYROLL system to explain how these symbols should be interpreted.

The logical design of PAYROLL and our example query correspond to symbols occurring at the top of the figure.

- S_L denotes a *logical vocabulary* and refers to 4 and 5.

- Σ denotes additional *logical constraints* on S_L and refers to 6 and 7.

- Q denotes a query on S_L, and can therefore refer to 14.

In turn, the above physical design for PAYROLL and example query plan now includes the remaining symbols at the middle and bottom of the figure.

- S_P denotes a *physical vocabulary* and refers to 8 and 9.

- Σ' denotes additional *physical constraints and interfaces* on S_P and refers to 10 and 11.

- Σ'' denotes constraints over $S_L \cup S_P$ that capture metadata that establishes a correspondence between logical and physical vocabulary and refers to 12 and 13.

- Q' denotes a query plan on S_P, and can therefore refer to 15.

Figure 1.1 also uses the symbol Σ as a way to refer to all constraints and interfaces in the context of a given query compilation problem. The intended interpretation of Σ will always be clear from context: as a set of logical constraints if we are discussing logical design, and as all constraints if we are discussing physical design.

With this notation and with this example scenario in mind, we now give a more concise definition of the subject of this book to summarize the notion of a logical design, the notion of a physical design and the problem of query compilation.

Definition 1.1   (Logical and physical design)   A *logical design* is given by a pair $\langle S_L, \Sigma \rangle$ consisting of a *logical vocabulary* S_L and a set of *logical constraints* Σ over S_L. A *physical design* is also given by a pair

$$\langle S_L \cup S_P, \Sigma = (\Sigma \cup \Sigma' \cup \Sigma'') \rangle .$$

This refines a logical design by adding a *physical vocabulary* S_P to a logical vocabulary S_L, and by adding a set of *physical constraints* $\Sigma' \cup \Sigma''$ over the resulting vocabulary to the set of logical constraints Σ. The physical constraints consist in turn of a set of constraints Σ' on the physical vocabulary S_P alone together with constraints Σ'' that establish a correspondence or mapping between S_L and S_P.   □

Definition 1.2   (Query compilation)   Given a physical design $\langle S_L \cup S_P, \Sigma \rangle$ and a query Q over the logical vocabulary S_L, find the best query plan Q' over the physical vocabulary S_P that correctly implements Q for any database that satisfies the additional constraints in Σ.   □

Both definitions serve only as a first cut since they leave many issues abstracted. Most importantly, this includes the choice of a language $\mathcal{L}$ for expressing a query Q or a query plan Q', and also for expressing the constraints and interfaces in Σ. This also includes what a database is and what it means for a query plan to "correctly implement" a query or, indeed, what it means to be a "best" query plan. In this book, these issues are resolved by adopting *first order logic* (FOL) as the choice for $\mathcal{L}$. Indeed, we shall see that FOL requires very little in the way of additional machinery to address all our requirements. For example, syntactic restrictions can be introduced to enable well-formed formulae in FOL to serve as a low-level plan language for query plans. This, in turn, enables *logical consequence* in FOL to fulfill a fundamental role in capturing what it means for a query plan to *implement* a user query.

There is another important observation about how we have defined the problem of query compilation that merits some discussion. In particular, we allow that it is possible that *no query plan exists for a given user query and physical design*. This happens when the physical design has insufficient material capabilities for computing answers to the user query. For example, the physical design might be "missing an access path" for some aspect of the logical design. Thus, a physical design is allowed to be incomplete with respect to its ability to compute the answers to an arbitrary user query. The appropriate response is to recognize such cases and report back that additional material capabilities are required. Note that existing relational database systems avoid this issue by creating, at the least,

Purely logical terms with no computational implications: entity, kind of entity, concept, attribute, attribute value, logical design, query.

Terms that have computational implications: file, record, record type, record address, field, B-tree, operation, field extraction, physical design, query plan.

More generic terms: information, data, metadata, sentence.

Figure 1.2: On terminology.

a default physical design. Presuming a default physical design, however, is inappropriate in cases where access to existing legacy sources must be integrated, and is therefore not presumed in this book.

In the next two chapters, we review how FOL can be used to formally capture logical and physical design, to express read only user queries, and, with a small number of extensions, read only query plans that implement user queries. We remind the reader that Appendix A provides a brief overview of FOL for readers who might require a review of basic material. Regardless, it is a good idea to read through Appendix A to review FOL terminology and the notation used in this book.

1.2 SUMMARY

We defined the terms *logical design*, *physical design* and *query compilation* by appealing to an example scenario for a hypothetical enterprise called ACME. In doing so, we have been careful to use nouns and noun phrases in both a consistent manner and that are most likely to match the readers expectations on their use in referring either to purely conceptual notions or to more concrete computational notions that touch on the topics of data encoding, data structures, and so on. A summary of our terminology and our intentions for this "mode of use" is given in Figure 1.2. For example, we assume that *entities* and *attribute values* are purely logical notions with no computational implications, whereas the opposite is true for *records* and *record fields*. For example, given the address of a record, one expects an operation that extracts the value of one of its fields is available, and that any invocation of this operation takes time bounded by a constant. Finally, we use the term *information* in a very general way to refer to both data and metadata that might in turn be either conceptual or concrete.

1.3 BIBLIOGRAPHIC NOTES

The notion of physical data independence was first proposed by Codd [1970] who used the simpler term *data independence*. A distinction between *logical* data independence and *physical* data independence was introduced later on by Date and Hopewell in a companion pair of papers, [Date and Hopewell, 1971a,b]. In defining physical data independence, Date and Hopewell implicitly attach a requirement that a physical design manifests sufficient material capabilities to enable at least one query plan for any possible query formulated in Codd's relational algebra. It is noteworthy that the origins of the related notion of *abstract data type* trace to roughly the same period [Parnas, 1972] (see Exercise 1.4).

1.4   EXERCISES WITH TOPICS FOR DISCUSSION

Exercise 1.3   Observe that there is no loop that calls the `emp-lookup` operation in the query plan 15 for our sample query 14, that there is no second call to `emp-lookup`. Write an essay that explains why this suffices in the context of PAYROLL metadata. What implications does this have on the requirements for a query compiler? More generally, how does this relate to the general issue of entity identity?

Exercise 1.4   The notion of an *abstract data type* is key part of the foundations of computer science. Write an essay that compares the notions of *physical data independence* and of *abstract data type*. How do they compare?

Exercise 1.5   Our characterization of a physical design as a refinement of logical design, by virtue of the addition of further vocabulary and constraints, suggests that personnel in ACME's DBA department have a more difficult job than personnel in ACME's APS department with regard to PAYROLL metadata. Indeed, the latter are only required to appreciate (but are responsible for) a strict "logical" subset of the metadata. However, the definition also suggests a way that designs can be organized in a hierarchy with more fundamental concepts defined in designs that occur closer to the root of the hierarchy, thus accommodating some form of *modularity* for metadata. Write an essay that explores this, considering, for example, whether such a hierarchy should have the form of a tree or more generally of a directed acyclic graph. How can such a hierarchy help to further reduce the overhead to train personnel? How could such a hierarchy be used to characterize a possibility for *logical data independence*?

Exercise 1.6   In our introductory comments, we characterized the notions of data and metadata as a "rough dichotomy" of information. Write an essay that considers general criteria for categorizing an arbitrary sentence as one that expresses either data or metadata. For example, one criteria might be the relative frequency of revision or update to a sentence in comparison to other sentences. Also consider the possibility that a sentence expresses information that should be categorized as both data and metadata. In this case, is it always possible to replace the sentence with two sentences that express strictly data and strictly metadata? And finally, consider extreme application scenarios in which all relevant information is only data or only metadata. Do such scenarios exist?

Exercise 1.7   Consider where ACME's APS department introduces another attribute for employee entities called `description` with the intention of capturing, for example, the following data.

> Mary's description is "Mary is one of our most productive
> employees in the more technical areas of the payroll system.
> Mary gets along extremely well with her colleagues, and is always
> punctual."

Observe how `description` values correspond to (possibly long) sequences of characters at one level, and to (unconstrained) English text at another. Now consider that a manager at ACME might be interested in finding answers to the following question.

> Find the `name` of each `employee` entity that would be a good choice to lead a project to incorporate recent changes to government regulations on income tax deductions in the PAYROLL system.

Write an essay on how the problems of physical design and query compilation, and also the problem of designing a language for expressing queries, are affected by this scenario. How do the consequences touch on the subject of *information retrieval*?

CHAPTER 2

Logical Design and User Queries

We now look into how first-order logic (FOL) can serve as the language for capturing metadata relating to logical design, and on how well-formed formulae in FOL can also serve as the language for expressing user queries. In doing so, we assume familiarity with the basic concepts and notation of FOL to the extent reviewed in Appendix A: how *formulae* are expressed, the notion of an *interpretation*, of a *valuation*, of *logical consequence*, and so on.

Our introductory comments in the first chapter have talked about how information can be partitioned into data and metadata. This distinction is realized in our use of FOL in the following way. First, the collection of all metadata for both logical and physical design will correspond to a choice of signature S in FOL together with a theory Σ over S that consists of closed formulae or sentences. Second, we assume that the collection of all data comprising a database corresponds *directly* to the notion of an interpretation $\mathcal{I}$ over the signature S. We also expect that $\mathcal{I}$, coupled with *any* valuation $\mathcal{V}$ over $\mathcal{I}$, is a model of the theory Σ, that the database $\mathcal{I}$ satisfies all sentences in Σ.

Viewing data in this way may seem confusing since the issue of how a database system references elements of the domain of $\mathcal{I}$, e.g., to communicate the results of evaluating queries, is left abstracted. It turns out that this is not really a problem if our main concern is on reasoning about design and about query compilation. However, in our summary comments, we comment on how this issue has traditionally been addressed in the context of relational databases: the *standard name assumption* to start with, and then the notions of *concrete domains*, of *closed world assumptions*, and so on.

2.1 LOGICAL DESIGN IN FOL

From Definition 1.1, a logical design is a pair consisting of a logical vocabulary S_L, that will now correspond to an FOL signature, coupled with logical constraints Σ over S_L, that will now correspond to an FOL theory over S_L. The following subsections consider choices for S_L and for Σ that relate to ACME's PAYROLL system.

2.1.1 LOGICAL VOCABULARIES

In FOL, logical database design begins by deciding on a signature that consists of a collection of predicate and function symbols appropriate to the application domain. We consider three options for the signature S_L appropriate to the logical database design of PAYROLL. In listing these options, we appeal to notation reviewed in Appendix A in which one writes P/n and f/n as shorthand to indicate that $Ar(P) = n$ or $Ar(f) = n$.

OPTION 1.

- $S_L^P = \{$employee$/3\}$, and
- $S_L^F = \emptyset$.

OPTION 2.

- $S_L^P = \{$employee$/1\}$, and
- $S_L^F = \{$employee-number$/1$, name$/1$, salary$/1\}$.

OPTION 3.

- $S_L^P = \{$employee$/1$, employee-number$/2$, name$/2$, salary$/2\}$.
- $S_L^F = \emptyset$.

The first option has the fewest non-logical parameters: a single 3-ary predicate is chosen with the intention of associating an employee name and salary, positions 2 and 3 of the predicate, with an employee-number, position 1 of the predicate. Note that position 1 serves a special role with this option in the sense that the set of employee number values in an interpretation $\mathcal{I}$ is identified with the set of employees. It is common in this case to say that the employee number value of a given 3-tuple in (employee)$^{\mathcal{I}}$ is a *visible object identifier* of some employee, and that the remaining two components of the 3-tuple express two facts about the employee.

The second option trades the need to remember the role of argument positions with the need to learn and remember additional non-logical parameters. The basic idea is to introduce unary predicates to capture the various kinds of entities, and to introduce unary functions to capture entity attributes. One particular advantage of this approach is that it separates entity classification from entity description: an entity e in a given interpretation $\mathcal{I}$ is an employee exactly when $e \in$ (employee)$^{\mathcal{I}}$, and all information about entities, such as a name or salary, is captured by unary functions. The second option also differs from the first in another way: it allows the possibility that more than one employee can have the same *combination* of values for attributes employee-number, name and salary (notwithstanding the role actually served by the first of these attributes). Proceeding in this manner with any n-ary predicate symbol is generally referred to as *reification*.

One disadvantage of the second option is that it now requires all entities to have a value for all attributes. The third option overcomes this requirement by replacing each unary function symbol with a new binary predicate symbol. This now makes it possible for an entity, including those that are employees, to have any number of employee numbers, names or salaries, including none. Indeed, replacing function symbols with new predicate symbols is always possible when a function-free signature is desired.

In summary, by a exhaustive use of reification, one can obtain a signature consisting of only unary predicate and function symbols, and by a subsequent replacement policy, by a signature consisting of only unary and binary predicate symbols.

2.1.2   LOGICAL CONSTRAINTS

In the following, we introduce sentences over the various options for S_L, ultimately leading to possible theories Σ over S_L that, when coupled with S_L, will constitute a logical design of PAYROLL. This is achieved by considering a progression of basic issues that relate to design, starting with the problem of identification.

Example 2.1   (On identifying entities)   Assume S_L is given by OPTION 1 above. The condition that *employees can be identified by their employee number* can be expressed as the FOL sentence

$$\forall x_1, x_2, y_1, y_2.(\exists z.(\texttt{employee}(z, x_1, x_2) \wedge \texttt{employee}(z, y_1, y_2))$$
$$\rightarrow ((x_1 \approx y_1) \wedge (x_2 \approx y_2))).$$

In effect, the sentence ensures that each employee is associated with a single 3-tuple in $(\texttt{employee})^{\mathcal{I}}$, that is, in any collection of data given by interpretation $\mathcal{I}$ for ACME's PAYROLL system. (Remember our introductory comments that the collection of all data corresponds to an interpretation.)

If S_L is given instead by OPTION 2, the same condition can be expressed as the FOL sentence

$$\forall x, y.($$
$$(\texttt{employee}(x) \wedge \texttt{employee}(y) \wedge \texttt{employee-number}(x) \approx \texttt{employee-number}(y))$$
$$\rightarrow x \approx y).$$

This sentence must be revised slightly for OPTION 3:

$$\forall x, y.($$
$$\exists z.(\texttt{employee}(x) \wedge \texttt{employee}(y)$$
$$\wedge \texttt{employee-number}(x, z) \wedge \texttt{employee-number}(y, z))$$
$$\rightarrow x \approx y).$$

More accurately, the revised sentence expresses the condition that *no pair of distinct employees may have any employee number at all in common* since it remains possible in OPTION 3 for employees to have any number of employee numbers.   □

Example 2.2   (On property functionality)   If OPTION 3 is chosen by ACME's APS department then it becomes necessary to disallow the number of possible values for an `employee-number`, `name`, or `salary` attribute for a given employee to exceed one. We therefore need to add constraints to the logical design that ensure these attributes are *partial functions*. Such constraints can be captured by adding the following three sentences to Σ:

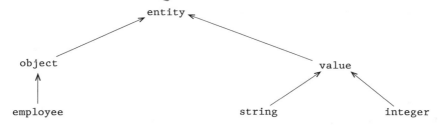

Figure 2.1: A simple taxonomy.

1. $\forall x, y.(\exists z.(\texttt{employee-number}(z, x) \wedge \texttt{employee-number}(z, y)) \rightarrow (x \approx y))$,

2. $\forall x, y.(\exists z.(\texttt{name}(z, x) \wedge \texttt{name}(z, y)) \rightarrow (x \approx y))$ and

3. $\forall x, y.(\exists z.(\texttt{salary}(z, x) \wedge \texttt{salary}(z, y)) \rightarrow (x \approx y))$.

$\square$

Our sentences have so far adhered to a pattern in which a consequence "forces" equality for a given pair of terms. In cases not relating to OPTION 2, the terms are function free. Such cases have desirable reasoning properties in query compilation and are called *equality generating dependencies* in the literature.

Definition 2.3   (Equality Generating Dependency)   Let ϕ denote a well-formed formula of the form $(\psi_1 \wedge \cdots \wedge \psi_m)$ in which each ψ_i is a function free atom. An *equality generating dependency (EGD)* is a sentence in FOL with the form

$$\forall x_1, x_2.(\exists x_3, \cdots, x_n.\phi \rightarrow (x_1 \approx x_2)) ,$$

where $n \geq 2$ and where $\mathsf{Fv}(\phi) = \{x_1, \ldots, x_n\}$.

$\square$

Example 2.4   (On taxonomies)   It is easy to capture basic taxonomic knowledge in FOL, an issue more clearly relevant to OPTIONS 2 and 3 for the signature $\mathsf{S_L}$ of ACME's PAYROLL system. In the following, we assume that deliberations by ACME's APS department on a classification of entities relevant to PAYROLL has resulted in the design of the simple taxonomy illustrated in Figure 2.1.

There are two immediate consequences on the logical design of PAYROLL. First, the figure suggests that the signature $\mathsf{S_L}$ should be revised by adding the unary predicates $\texttt{entity}$, $\texttt{object}$, $\texttt{value}$, $\texttt{string}$ and $\texttt{integer}$ to $\mathsf{S_L^P}$. Second, the overall shape of the figure suggests sentences should then be added to the logical design of PAYROLL as follows:

1. *Everything is an entity*,

$$\forall x.\texttt{entity}(x);$$

2. *More specific entities are objects and values,*

$$\forall x.(\texttt{object}(x) \rightarrow \texttt{entity}(x))$$

and

$$\forall x.(\texttt{value}(x) \rightarrow \texttt{entity}(x))$$

(note that both sentences are logical consequences of all things being entities);

3. *More specific objects are employees,*

$$\forall x.(\texttt{employee}(x) \rightarrow \texttt{object}(x))$$

and

4. *More specific values are strings and integers,*

$$\forall x.(\texttt{string}(x) \rightarrow \texttt{value}(x))$$

and

$$\forall x.(\texttt{integer}(x) \rightarrow \texttt{value}(x)) \,.$$

This level of detail might seem to be overkill for the OPTION 1 signature in which there is no need for *employee objects* in the domain of any interpretation $\mathcal{I}$ that are separate from so-called *atomic* values such as integers or strings. Indeed, an OPTION 1 *style* for logical design reflects a philosophy in which all entities are considered to be values—a *purely relational* perspective in which non-values, such as the general notion of an *entity* or an *object*, are left abstracted and are not required to occur in the domain of an interpretation.

Figure 2.1, together with our intuitions, also suggest that *nothing is just an entity* and also that *nothing is just a value* (at least in regard to the PAYROLL system). Such conditions are commonly referred to as *cover constraints* in the literature, and are captured by the pair of sentences

$$\forall x.(\texttt{entity}(x) \rightarrow (\texttt{object}(x) \vee \texttt{value}(x)))$$

and

$$\forall x.(\texttt{value}(x) \rightarrow (\texttt{string}(x) \vee \texttt{integer}(x))) \,.$$

In general, cover constraints require sentences that employ disjunction.

And finally, Figure 2.1, again together with our intuitions, suggest that *objects are distinct from values*, and that *strings are distinct from integers*. Such conditions in this case are commonly referred to as *disjointness constraints* in the literature, and are in turn captured by the pair of sentences

$$\forall x.(\texttt{object}(x) \rightarrow \neg\texttt{value}(x))$$

and

$$\forall x.(\texttt{string}(x) \rightarrow \neg\texttt{integer}(x)) \,.$$

In general, disjointness constraints require sentences that employ (some form of) negation.   □

Example 2.5   (On attribute typing)   The above taxonomy introduces a number of additional unary predicates in ACME's PAYROLL signature that can be used to ensure that attribute values are of appropriate types. Sentences that express such typing constraints for each of our possible PAYROLL signatures are given as follows: for OPTION 1,

$$\forall x, y, z.(\texttt{employee}(x, y, z) \to (\texttt{integer}(x) \land \texttt{string}(y) \land \texttt{integer}(z)));$$

for OPTION 2,

$$\forall x.(\texttt{employee}(x) \to (\texttt{integer}(\texttt{employee-number}(x))$$
$$\land \ \texttt{string}(\texttt{name}(x))$$
$$\land \ \texttt{integer}(\texttt{salary}(x))));$$

and for OPTION 3,

$$\forall x.(\texttt{employee}(x) \to \exists y, z, w.(\texttt{employee-number}(x, y) \land \texttt{integer}(y)$$
$$\land \ \texttt{name}(x, z) \land \texttt{string}(z))$$
$$\land \ \texttt{salary}(x, w) \land \texttt{integer}(w))).$$

Finally, by choosing OPTION 3 as our logical signature, it becomes possible to express that *only employees have employee numbers*:

$$\forall x.(\exists y.\texttt{employee-number}(x, y) \to \texttt{employee}(x)).$$

Similar sentences would need to be added to Σ if the APS department should decide that only an employee may also have a name or a salary.   □

With the exception of cover and disjointness constraints when defining taxonomies, all the remaining sentences above adhere to a different pattern in which a consequence now "forces" the existence of one or more tuples. Again, the cases not relating to OPTION 2 (in which terms are function free) are singled out in the literature (because of desirable reasoning properties in query compilation) and are called *tuple generating dependencies*.

Definition 2.6   (Tuple Generating Dependency)   Let ϕ and ψ denote well-formed formulae with the respective forms $(\phi_1 \land \cdots \land \phi_m)$ and $(\psi_1 \land \cdots \land \psi_n)$ in which each ϕ_i and ψ_i is a function free atom. A *tuple generating dependency (TGD)* is a sentence in FOL with the form

$$\forall x_1, \cdots, x_i.(\exists y_1, \cdots, y_j.\phi \to \exists z_1, \cdots, z_k.\psi) \,,$$

where $\textsf{Fv}(\phi)$ and $\textsf{Fv}(\psi)$ are the respective sets $\{x_1, \ldots, x_i\} \cup \{y_1, \ldots, y_j\}$ and $\{x_1, \ldots, x_i\} \cup \{z_1, \ldots, z_k\}$. A *full* TGD satisfies the additional condition that $k = 0$, that $\textsf{Fv}(\psi) = \{x_1, \ldots, x_i\}$.   □

Observe that many of the above sentences in FOL that are TGDs are also full TGDs. Also observe that, with the exception of cover and disjointness constraints, the first and third options for the logical design $\langle \Sigma, S_L \rangle$ of ACME's PAYROLL system consist entirely of either EGDs or TGDs.

2.2   USER QUERIES IN FOL

We begin by formally defining user queries and their evaluation. When reading through the definition, remember that we assume the collection of all *data* for a database corresponds to an interpretation of a given signature, and that this interpretation is a model of all sentences that comprise the logical constraints over the signature.

Definition 2.7   (User Queries)   (*query syntax*) Let S denote a signature in FOL. A *user query Q* over S is a well-formed formula in WFF(S) *with defined parameters* that correspond to a possibly empty subset of Fv(Q), denoted Param(Q). Q is a *conjunctive query* if it also has the form

$$\exists x_1. \cdots . \exists x_m . (\psi_1 \wedge \cdots \wedge \psi_n)$$

in which each ψ_i is a function free atom. Q is a *positive query* if it has the form

$$Q_1 \vee \ldots \vee Q_l \, ,$$

where each Q_i is a conjunctive query for which Fv(Q_i) = Fv(Q). Finally, we write $Q\{x_1, \ldots, x_n\}$ as shorthand to indicate that Param(Q) = $\{x_1, \ldots, x_n\}$, or more simply just Q if Param(Q) = $\emptyset$.

(*query semantics*) Let $\mathcal{I}$ denote an interpretation of S. The *evaluation of Q with respect to $\mathcal{I}$*, written $Q(\mathcal{I})$, is given by

$$\{\langle \mathcal{V}(x_1), \ldots, \mathcal{V}(x_n)\rangle \in (\Delta^{\mathcal{I}})^n \mid \mathcal{I}, \mathcal{V} \models Q\},$$

where $(x_1, \ldots, x_n)$ where is the lexicographic ordering of Fv(Q).   □

Thus, a given n-tuple $\langle e_1, \ldots, e_n \rangle \in (\Delta^{\mathcal{I}})^n$ occurs in the evaluation of a user query Q with respect to an interpretation $\mathcal{I}$ if and only if there exists a valuation $\mathcal{V}$ over $\mathcal{I}$ such that

$$\mathcal{I}, \mathcal{V}[x_1 \mapsto e_1] \cdots [x_n \mapsto e_n] \models Q,$$

where $(x_1, \ldots, x_n)$ is the lexicographic ordering of the variables in Fv(Q). Notice that this semantics does not rely on which of its free variables also occurs in Param(Q), that is, on which of its free variables are parameters to the query. Rather, this distinction is necessary to enable a user to inform a query compiler that it must find an efficient plan to evaluate the query when particular entities in an interpretation are supplied *as parameters* for the variables in Param(Q).

We return to ACME's PAYROLL system for examples of user queries. Our examples illustrate the use of progressively richer subsets of the logical parameters of FOL.

Example 2.8   (Using conjunction and existention quantification)   Recall our original example of a user query on PAYROLL from the first chapter:

Find the `salary` *for any* `employee` *whose* `employee-number` *is given by a parameter p.*

Assuming that a salary value is determined by variable x, the query is specified as follows: for OPTION 1,

$$\exists y.\texttt{employee}(p, y, x)\{p\}$$

(recall that the sequence of argument positions corresponds to employee numbers, names and salaries); for OPTION 2,

$$\exists y.(\texttt{employee}(y) \wedge (\texttt{employee-number}(y) \approx p) \wedge (\texttt{salary}(y) \approx x))\{p\};$$

and for OPTION 3,

$$\exists y.(\texttt{employee}(y) \wedge \texttt{employee-number}(y, p) \wedge \texttt{salary}(y, x))\{p\}.$$

For any of these options, the evaluation of the query with respect to some interpretation $\mathcal{I}$ will correspond to a binary relation r over $\Delta^{\mathcal{I}}$. Since the lexicographic ordering of the free variables for each of the above is (p, x), the queries also express the requirement that a query plan must be found that will efficiently enumerate the 2-tuples $\langle e_1, e_2 \rangle$ occurring in r for which e_1 matches a given parameter. Finally, observe that the first and third formulations are also *conjunctive queries*. □

Example 2.9   (Using conjunction, disjunction and existential quantification)   Now suppose ACME's APS department also needs to express the query:

Find the `employee-number` x *for any* `employee` *that has a* `salary` *matching either the parameter p_1 or the parameter p_2.*

The query is specified as follows: for OPTION 1,

$$(\exists y.\texttt{employee}(x, y, p_1) \vee \exists z.\texttt{employee}(x, z, p_2))\{p_1, p_2\};$$

for OPTION 2,

$$($$
$$\exists y.(\texttt{employee}(y) \wedge (\texttt{salary}(y) \approx p_1) \wedge (\texttt{employee-number}(y) \approx x)) \vee$$
$$\exists z.(\texttt{employee}(z) \wedge (\texttt{salary}(z) \approx p_2) \wedge (\texttt{employee-number}(z) \approx x))$$
$$)\{p_1, p_2\};$$

and for OPTION 3,

$$($$
$$\exists y.(\texttt{employee}(y) \wedge \texttt{salary}(y, p_1) \wedge \texttt{employee-number}(y, x)) \vee$$
$$\exists z.(\texttt{employee}(z) \wedge \texttt{salary}(z, p_2) \wedge \texttt{employee-number}(z, x))$$
$$)\{p_1, p_2\}.$$

Observe for this query that each of the options requires the use of disjunction to express the user's query intent, that it is no longer possible to express this intent by using only conjunctive and existential quantification. Also observe that the first and third formulations are also *positive queries*.   □

Example 2.10   (Using conjunction, negation and existential quantification)   Finally, suppose the APS department needs to express the query:

> Find the `employee-number` x *for any* `employee` *that has a* `name` *that is also unique.*

This query is specified as follows: for OPTION 1,

$$\exists y_1, y_2.(\text{employee}(x, y_1, y_2) \wedge \neg \exists z_1, z_2.(\text{employee}(z_1, y_1, z_2) \wedge \neg (x \approx z_1)));$$

for OPTION 2,

$$\exists y.(\text{employee}(y) \wedge (\text{employee-number}(y) \approx x) \\ \wedge \neg \exists z.(\text{employee}(z) \wedge \neg (y \approx z) \wedge (\text{name}(y) \approx \text{name}(z))));$$

and for OPTION 3,

$$\exists y.(\text{employee}(y) \wedge \text{employee-number}(y, x)) \\ \wedge \neg \exists z, w.(\text{employee}(z) \wedge \neg (y \approx z) \wedge \text{name}(y, w) \wedge \text{name}(z, w)).$$

For this query, each of the options requires the use of negation to express the user's query intent. Indeed, the full power of FOL is required.   □

The above examples show that the three options we examined express essentially the same logical designs. Hence, for the remainder of the book, we consider only the options for both logical and physical design that are *relational* in nature, that is, for which all signatures are function free. This simplifies our presentation without any loss of generality since it is straightforward to replace a function symbol f in a given FOL theory with a new predicate symbol P in which $\text{Ar}(P) = \text{Ar}(f) + 1$ and then adding constraints to express typing and functionality constraints on any interpretations of P.

2.3   SUMMARY

We have seen how logical design for a database can be naturally formulated as sentences in FOL, and that a large part of logical design corresponds to equality and tuple generating dependencies. This will prove useful in Chapter 5 where we review chase procedures that have been developed to help compile user queries.

The evaluation of a user query is defined as a set of n-tuples over the underlying domain of an interpretation. As mentioned in our introductory comments, this leaves open the issue of how such results might be materially conveyed to application programs, indeed, how our semantic notion of a query result tuple t can be converted to a syntactic notion of t. A simple and common approach to settling the issue is to adopt the so-called *standard name assumption* whereby the domain of an interpretation effectively augments a signature by an additional set of *standard names* for each of its elements. Thus, each component of a result tuple t is simply mapped to its standard name, thereby obtaining a syntactic (and therefore communicable) form for t.

The standard name assumption requires that the signature is determined in two phases that precede and follow the selection of an interpretation. Since this is a significant deviation from FOL, researchers have investigated alternative approaches in which data, like metadata, is captured in the form of sentences in FOL and in which the result of a user query is defined with respect to logical consequence. This has led to a number of insights on the nature of theories that are required in order for this to work.

- Such theories require the prior introduction of *concrete domains* in which a "starting" signature is presumed, e.g., a countably infinite set of constant symbols denoting finite length strings together with a countably infinite starting set of sentences that enforce a *unique name assumption* whereby distinct constant symbols must denote distinct elements in any interpretation.

- For the results of queries, as we have defined them, to be defined by logical consequence, it becomes necessary to augment a theory to effectively force a unique interpretation for non-logical parameters. This is accomplished by a combination of sentences: 1) a finite set of ground atoms for n-tuples occurring in the interpretation of predicates, and 2) manifesting *closed world assumptions* that such n-tuples are an exhaustive (finite) enumeration of predicate interpretations (see references to the work by Reiter below).

Modern user query languages such as SQL have several features that are not captured by our definition of a user query. In this next chapter, we introduce a plan language for expressing query plans in which we address two of these features relating to query evaluation: 1) that results are guaranteed to be finite, and 2) that results may have duplicates. Although the latter feature is debatable in the context of user queries, it is essential in the context of query plans in which allowing duplicates in intermediate results is often crucial to performance. In Chapter 4, we also show how it becomes possible in our framework to support null values with so-called *null inapplicable* semantics, a capability that is often crucial in physical design.

However, there are two categories of SQL features that are beyond the scope of this book.

- We do not attempt to address the possibility that the result of a user query has a meaningful order. This becomes important when it is necessary to rank the n-tuples comprising the result, or when a lengthy printed report must be produced that enables efficient manual search. Ordering can also be an important issue in choosing a query plan to implement a user query, e.g., in knowing when merge joins that avoid sort costs are possible.

- We do not attempt to address second order features, e.g., that compute transitive closures or that require reasoning about aggregate functions that perform counting or summing.

2.4 BIBLIOGRAPHIC NOTES

The relational model of data was first proposed by Codd [1970]. Specifically, Codd showed how a logical design can be viewed as a finite selection of non-logical parameters corresponding to predicate symbols of arbitrary arity, and how databases could be viewed as interpretations in which the predicate symbols denote finite relations. Codd also introduced the notions of *primary keys* and a *normal form* in which tuples are viewed as encoding simple facts about objects identified by primary key values. Concern with logical modeling blossomed thereafter with a number of authors proposing a variety of so-called *semantic data models* and then *object-oriented databases*, see Tsichritzis and Lochovsky [1982] and Kim [1990] for respective surveys. Perhaps the most influential of this work was a paper by Chen [1976] in which he proposed the *entity relationship model*.

Our assumption that data corresponds directly to an interpretation in FOL was recognized early on by Reiter who introduced the notions of *closed* and *open world assumptions* [Reiter, 1977] and demonstrated how an FOL signature and theory would need to be augmented to reduce query evaluation with the closed world assumption to logical consequence [Reiter, 1980].

Tuple and equality generating dependencies were proposed by Beeri and Vardi [1984] as a fragment of FOL that sufficed to abstract a large variety of relational constraints that were developed in the 1970s and early 1980s following Codd's introduction of the relational model. Notably, this included *functional dependencies* [Codd, 1971], a useful and natural generalization of keys, and *inclusion dependencies* [Casanova et al., 1984].

A concurrent effort on suitable ways of capturing metadata has been ongoing in the area of knowledge representation in artificial intelligence since the 1960s. Early work on *semantic network models* and *terminological logics* merged by the mid-1990s into the topic of *description logics* [Baader et al., 2007] which are largely fragments of FOL with desirable computational properties (see Exercise 2.3). Notably, such logics underlie recent efforts on developing ontology languages for web-based data [OWL 2 Web Ontology Language: New Features and Rational, 2009].

2.5 EXERCISES WITH TOPICS FOR DISCUSSION

Exercise 2.1   Explore how our user queries and query semantics might be embellished to enable users to express ordering and ranking criteria. One complication with the current semantics is a consequence of not imposing any conditions on an interpretation beyond the fact that it satisfies a logical design. This make it possible for the number of n-tuples comprising the evaluation of a query to not be finite. (Indeed, there are practical situations in the context of so-called *streaming databases* in which this is desirable.)

Exercise 2.2   Explore applications for ACME's `payroll` system in which *genuine joins* are needed. A genuine join happens in a user query Q when Q does not require a meaningful semantic relationship between two of its free variables, such as in the case of user query

$$\exists u, v, w.(\texttt{employee}(x, u, v)) \wedge \texttt{employee}(y, w, v)).$$

An evaluation of this query will denote all pairs of `employee-number` values for employees that have only a tenuous relationship to each other: that so happen to have the same salary.

Exercise 2.3   *Description logics* (DLs) are largely fragments of FOL that are variable free and have desirable computational properties. They were developed to capture ontological knowledge. Explore how the notion of an *ontology* compares to the notion of a *logical design* or *database schema*, and consider in particular how various DL dialects can be used to capture the logical design of a database.

Exercise 2.4   A user query is *domain independent* if its evaluation with respect to any interpretation $\mathcal{I}_1$ coincides with its evaluation with respect to any other interpretation $\mathcal{I}_2$ whenever $\mathcal{I}_1$ and $\mathcal{I}_2$ agree on their interpretations of all non-logical parameters. What is the computational complexity of determining if an arbitrary user query is domain independent? Explore syntactic restrictions of user queries that express exactly the class of domain independent user queries. (Hint: consider textbook presentations of the *relational algebra*.)

CHAPTER 3

Basic Physical Design and Query Plans

Starting in this chapter, we consider physical design and how to express plans to evaluate queries over physical design. This is accomplished incrementally, beginning with a focus on basic data structures such as arrays, linked lists and simple search trees. We also introduce a plan language for expressing query plans in terms of the fundamental capabilities that underlie such structures. In the next chapter, we show how this plan language together with basic data structures can be composed in various ways to capture more sophisticated data structures involving such artifacts as hashing, user defined functions, two-level store, and so on.

FOL continues to serve a central role: it will now function as the primary vehicle for capturing metadata relating to physical design and as a way to understand how query plans implement user queries. In particular, we consider how to express physical design in FOL, showing how such design can be captured in terms of a physical vocabulary coupled with various constraints and simple interfaces that are almost entirely given in terms of signatures and well-formed formulae.

ACME's PAYROLL system also continues to serve as our running example for illustrative purposes. In this chapter, we focus our attention on the logical designs of PAYROLL corresponding to OPTION 1 and OPTION 3 introduced in the previous chapter. Recall that the PAYROLL logical vocabulary for the former consisted of a single 3-ary employee predicate symbol and for the latter as the FOL signature S_L with

- $S_L^P = \{$employee/1, employee-number/2, name/2, salary/2$\}$ and

- $S_L^F = \emptyset$.

This option was obtained from OPTION 2 by replacing three unary function symbols with three binary predicate symbols. Also recall from the previous chapter how logical constraints were then formulated to ensure that the interpretation of the three binary predicate symbols behave as unary total functions over employee entities.

In the first section, we introduce the notion of an *access path* to serve as the link between basic data structures and the underlying capabilities manifest by such structures. This leads to the first construct in our query plan language for expressing *atomic query plans* that realize "black box" scanning and searching functionality. The next section more carefully defines what it means to *execute* a query plan and what it means for a query plan to *implement* a user query. The final section introduces the remaining operators for our plan language in an incremental fashion, starting with the introduction of operations that can express conjunctive query plans.

3.1   ACCESS PATHS AND SIMPLE SCANNING

Assume that ACME's DBA department has settled on a very simple physical design for PAYROLL in which all employee information is recorded in a main-memory array. Pseudo-code declaring this array, in some suitable global context, might be given as follows:

```
array emp-array [1 to n] of
    integer emp-salary
    integer emp-num
    string  emp-name.
```

Our intention is that the `salary`, `employee-number` and `name` of each `employee` is recorded at some position i in the array in corresponding fields. Also assume the DBA department ensures that the array entries are ordered by a major sort on `emp-salary` values and by a minor sort on `emp-num` values. This will ensure that lower `salary` values occur earlier in the array, and for a subrange recording employee information for employees having a particular salary, lower `employee-number` values occur earlier.

To capture this physical design in FOL, one thinks in terms of *capabilities*. In particular, the design implies an ability to efficiently do each of the following, which is then "recognized" by introducing a new predicate symbol:

1. the symbol `emp-array0/3` to capture the ability to scan all entries in `emp-array`;

2. the symbol `emp-array1/3` to capture the ability to scan all entries in `emp-array` with the first field matching a given `salary` value; and

3. the symbol `emp-array2/3` to capture the ability to find an entry in `emp-array` with the first and second fields matching a given `salary` value and a given `employee-number` value, respectively.

One must assume that the DBA department provides the code that *implements* these capabilities in a library or at runtime, for example, code that performs a binary search of `emp-array` in the case of `emp-array1` and `emp-array2`.

Recall from the first chapter that the new `emp-array`i predicate symbols are part of the *physical vocabulary* S_P for PAYROLL. To distinguish these predicate symbols with their material capabilities, we refine FOL signatures by introducing the notion of an *access path* and its *binding pattern*. Also, as one might expect with basic data structures such as `emp-array`, any interpretation of these predicate symbols should be *finite* for any particular combination of input parameters (more on this later on in the chapter).

Definition 3.1   (Access Paths and Binding Patterns)   Let S denote an FOL signature. The *access paths* of S form a distinguished subset S_A of the predicate symbols S_P comprising the physical vocabulary of S. The *binding pattern* of an access path $P \in S_A$, denoted $Bp(P)$, is a non-negative integer satisfying $0 \leq Bp(P) \leq Ar(P)$. We write $P/n/m$ to indicate that P is a predicate symbol with arity n and that P is also an access path with binding pattern m (and write $P/n/m \in S_A$).   □

Thus, the declaration of `emp-array` is captured by adding the set of access paths

$$\{\texttt{emp-array0}/3/0, \texttt{emp-array1}/3/1, \texttt{emp-array2}/3/2\}$$

to S_A. Again, from our definitions, and as illustrated in Figure 1.1, this new set of predicate symbols is now the *physical vocabulary* S_P of ACME's PAYROLL system.

The notion of an access path makes it possible to capture basic query plans that express the idea of *scanning a collection type* as simple atomic formulae in FOL. In particular, the simple mention of an access path serves as the first construct in our plan language. We consider examples relating to our `emp-array`i access paths that capture the material capabilities that underlie the `emp-array` pseudo-code.

Example 3.2   (File scan)   Consider where ACME's APS department needs a plan for the query:

Report all information about each `employee`.

Given the logical design of PAYROLL based on OPTION 1, this can be expressed as the user query:

$$\texttt{employee}(x, y, z)$$

assuming x, y and z correspond, respectively, to values for an `employee-number`, a `name` and a `salary`. For the OPTION 3 design, the query is instead:

$$\exists u.(\texttt{employee}(u) \land \texttt{employee-number}(u, x) \land \texttt{name}(u, y) \land \texttt{salary}(u, z)).$$

(Recall from our conventions that, since there is no indication otherwise, there are no query parameters in either case.) An efficient query plan that implements these queries can now be given by an atomic formula in which the predicate is also an access path:

$$\texttt{emp-array0}(z, x, y).$$

We refer to such a plan as an *atomic query plan*. In the database literature, such a plan is often called a *file scan*, in part to emphasize that the plan entails an exhaustive enumeration of some collection type (in this case, an array).

So how might it be possible for a query compiler to find such a plan for either formulation of the user query? Recall from Figure 1.1 that this will require ACME's DBA group to specify *mapping* or *correspondence* constraints Σ over the signature $(S_L \cup S_P)$. Such constraints provide the necessary "connections" for possible interpretations $\mathcal{I}$ (encoding factual data) of the *logical vocabulary* $\mathsf{S_L}$ and the *physical vocabulary* $\mathsf{S_P}$ of PAYROLL. With OPTION I for $\mathsf{S_L}$, this would be easily accomplished by including the sentence

$$\forall x, y, z.(\texttt{employee}(x, y, z) \rightarrow \texttt{emp-array0}(z, x, y))$$

and the sentence

$$\forall x, y, z.(\texttt{emp-array0}(z, x, y) \rightarrow \texttt{employee}(x, y, z))$$

in Σ. (Note that each of these sentences is a full TGD.)   □

A query plan Q in our plan language will always define a set of *input variables* and a disjoint set of *output variables*, denoted $\mathsf{In}(Q)$ and $\mathsf{Out}(Q)$, respectively. We will also be careful to say how Q maps to a user query, denoted $\mathsf{Uq}(Q)$. This mapping will enable us to say how query plans *implement* user queries by appealing mainly to logical consequence in FOL.

Definition 3.3 (Atomic Query Plans)   Let S denote an FOL signature. The first production of a grammar that defines the *query plans* induced by S, denoted $\mathsf{PLAN(S)}$, is given as follows:

- $Q ::= P(x_1, \ldots, x_m, x_{m+1}, \ldots, x_n)$ (where $x_i \in V$ and $P/n/m \in \mathsf{S_A}$).

Note that we overload our notation by also using Q, possibly subscripted, to refer to elements of $\mathsf{PLAN(S)}$ as well as to user queries. A plan Q obtained by this single production is called an *atomic query plan* and has *input variables* $\mathsf{In}(Q)$ and *output variables* $\mathsf{Out}(Q)$ given by $\{x_1, \ldots, x_m\}$ and $\{x_{m+1}, \ldots, x_n\}$, respectively. The *user query mapping* of Q, denoted $\mathsf{Uq}(Q)$, is Q itself, where $\mathsf{Param}(Q) = \{x_1, \ldots, x_m\}$.   □

Returning to our example of a file scan of `emp-array`, since $\mathsf{Bp}(\texttt{emp-array0}) = 0$, there are no *input variables* for the atomic query plan. In contrast, the set $\{x, y, z\}$ corresponds to the *output variables* of this plan, and the plan itself maps to the user query

$$\texttt{emp-array0}(z, x, y)\{\} .$$

(This time, we have taken care to indicate that there are no query parameters.)

Example 3.4 (Index scan)   Consider where the APS department has a second query for which a plan is required:

> *Report all information about each* `employee` *that has a given* `salary`.

Again, assuming that x, y and z correspond to values for an `employee-number`, a `name` and a `salary`, this is formulated in terms of a user query for `Option 1` as:

$$\texttt{employee}(x, y, z)\{z\};$$

and for `Option` 3 as:

$$\exists u.(\texttt{employee}(u) \wedge \texttt{employee-number}(u, x) \wedge \texttt{name}(u, y) \wedge \texttt{salary}(u, z))\{z\}.$$

An efficient query plan for these queries can use the `emp-array1` access path:

$$\texttt{emp-array1}(z, x, y).$$

In this case, since $\texttt{Bp}(\texttt{emp-array1}) = 1$, the plan can only be used when a value is supplied for the first parameter of the atomic formula. Thus, the input variables for this plan are given by the set $\{z\}$ and the output variables by the set $\{x, y\}$. Of course, this all makes sense because the major sort of array `emp-array` on the first field of its elements enables ACME's DBA department to provide library or runtime code "implementing" `emp-array1` by performing a binary search of `emp-array`.

In the database literature, such a plan is called an *index scan*, in part to emphasize that the plan entails an enumeration of the elements of an index that satisfies a search condition for the index, such as in the case of an ordered array. □

Example 3.5 (Index lookup)   Finally, consider a third query by the APS department:

Report the name of any `employee` *that has a given* `salary` *and* `employee-number`.

With the same choices for variable names, this is formulated as the user query

$$\texttt{employee}(x, y, z)\{x, z\}$$

for OPTION 1, and the user query

$$\exists u.(\texttt{employee}(u) \wedge \texttt{employee-number}(u, x) \wedge \texttt{name}(u, y) \wedge \texttt{salary}(u, z))\{x, z\}$$

for OPTION 3. An efficient query plan for these queries would use the `emp-array2` access path:

$$\texttt{emp-array2}(z, x, y).$$

The input and output variables in this case are given by the respective sets $\{x, z\}$ and $\{y\}$ since $\texttt{Bp}(\texttt{emp-array2}) = 2$.

This kind of plan is more often called an *index lookup* in the database literature, in preference to an index scan, to bring attention to the fact that at most a single result will be returned by the scan. This makes sense for access path `emp-array2` since logical design for PAYROLL prohibits any pair of distinct `employee` entities from sharing the same value for their `employee-number`. □

It is important to understand that the code for each of these atomic query plans must be provided by ACME's DBA department. In the case of access path `emp-array0`, this pre-existing code might hypothetically be given by the following pseudo-code. The code provides an ability to scan `emp-array` by a simple `first/next` protocol.

```
function emp-array0-first              function emp-array0-next
    i := 0                                 i := i + 1
    return emp-array0-next                 if (i > n) return false
                                           x₁ := emp-array[i].emp-salary
                                           x₂ := emp-array[i].emp-num
                                           x₃ := emp-array[i].emp-name
                                           return true
```

The protocol assumes access to a global state that records bindings for variables x_1, x_2 and x_3 in order to communicate the contents of `emp-array`. As might be expected for data structures that correspond to collection types (such as arrays), such a state also requires the introduction of additional variables to record scanning status (such as variable i).

Our examples of atomic query plans are based on using an array as a basic collection type. This provided the motivation for introducing access paths as the means of capturing basic scanning and searching capabilities manifest by such types. Alternatives to an array could also have served the same purpose, such as linked lists, simple search trees and so on. It is beyond the scope of this book to consider the synthesis of such data structures as part of the job of query compilation. However, in the next chapter, we shall see how physical design based on more sophisticated data structures can be usefully decomposed into simpler data structures with relationships that *can* be captured in FOL to an extent that makes it completely unnecessary to provide explicit `first/next` code for the former. Indeed, such "decomposition" of more complex data structures can enable compilation opportunities that would otherwise not be possible. The lesson is that, once given `first/next` "black box" code for the basic data structures such as records, arrays, linked lists and simple search trees, constraints can be then be expressed in FOL that do the rest.

3.2 QUERY PLAN EXECUTION

The following pseudo-code illustrates how, in general, a query plan Q, embodied by functions Q-first and Q-next, might be embedded in application code, in this case, a program that simply *prints a line* for each result computed by Q:

$$
\begin{aligned}
&\texttt{if } Q\texttt{-first} \\
&\quad \texttt{repeat} \\
&\qquad \texttt{printline("} x_1 \texttt{"} = x_1, \ \ldots, \ \texttt{"} x_n \texttt{"} = x_m) \\
&\quad \texttt{until not } Q\texttt{-next,}
\end{aligned}
\tag{3.1}
$$

where $\{x_1, \ldots, x_m\}$ are the input and output variables of Q. For example, if Q corresponds to the query plan above that performs a file scan,

$$\text{emp-array0}(x_3, x_1, x_2),$$

and if the database is given by interpretation $\mathcal{I}$, then running this code would have the effect of producing the output

$$x_1 = e_{1,1}, \quad x_2 = e_{1,2}, \quad x_3 = e_{1,3}$$
$$x_1 = e_{2,1}, \quad x_2 = e_{2,2}, \quad x_3 = e_{2,3}$$
$$\vdots$$
$$x_1 = e_{n,1}, \quad x_2 = e_{n,2}, \quad x_3 = e_{n,3},$$

that is, of printing the contents of each of the n elements of array emp-array effectively given by $\mathcal{I}$, in particular, where $e_{i,1}$ (resp. $e_{i,2}$, $e_{i,3}$) are emp-num values (resp. emp-name and emp-salary values) in $\Delta^{\mathcal{I}}$ for each row i occurring in the output.

In general, the ith line produced by (3.1) reports the current binding of input and output variables $\{x_1, \ldots, x_m\}$ in some global state that would be produced by an invocation of function Q-first followed by $i - 1$ invocations of function Q-next. Assuming the initial values for the *input variables* of Q are provided by a valuation $\mathcal{V}$, we capture this behavior as follows.

Definition 3.6 (Query Plan Execution) Let Q be a query plan with input and output variables $\{x_1, \ldots, x_m\}$, $\mathcal{I}$ an interpretation and $\mathcal{V}$ a valuation over $\mathcal{I}$. (Assume $\mathcal{V}(x)$, where x is an input variable of Q, corresponds to the value of x supplied as input to a particular execution of Q.) We write $\text{Size}(Q, \mathcal{I}, \mathcal{V})$ to denote the number of lines of output produced by running (3.1) above, write $\text{Line}_i(Q, \mathcal{I}, \mathcal{V})$ to denote the valuation

$$\mathcal{V}[x_1 \mapsto e_{i,1}] \cdots [x_m \mapsto e_{i,m}]$$

derived from $\mathcal{V}$ as prescribed by the ith line of this output, and write $\text{Exec}(Q, \mathcal{I}, \mathcal{V})$ as shorthand for

$$\{\text{Line}_i(Q, \mathcal{I}, \mathcal{V}) \mid 1 \leq i \leq \text{Size}(Q, \mathcal{I}, \mathcal{V})\}.$$

We say that *Q produces a set relative to $\mathcal{I}$ and $\mathcal{V}$* if

$$\text{Size}(Q, \mathcal{I}, \mathcal{V}) = |\text{Exec}(Q, \mathcal{I}, \mathcal{V})|.$$

$\square$

This way of understanding query plan execution enables us to characterize important properties relating to query plans and interpretations.

Definition 3.7 (Termination, Soundness, and Completeness of Query Plans) Let S denote an FOL signature, $\mathcal{I}$ an interpretation of S and Q a query plan in PLAN(S). Q is *terminating*, *sound* and *complete relative to $\mathcal{I}$* if the following respective conditions are satisfied:

- (*terminating*) for any valuation $\mathcal{V}$ over $\mathcal{I}$, an execution of the pseudo-code given by (3.1) above terminates after printing a finite number of lines;

- (*sound*) for any valuation $\mathcal{V}$ over $\mathcal{I}$ and any line i obtained by an execution of (3.1) above,

$$\mathcal{I}, \mathsf{Line}_i(Q, \mathcal{I}, \mathcal{V}) \models \mathsf{Uq}(Q);$$

and

- (*complete*) for any valuation $\mathcal{V}$ over $\mathcal{I}$ such that $\mathcal{I}, \mathcal{V} \models \mathsf{Uq}(Q)$, there exists a valuation $\mathcal{V}'$ over $\mathcal{I}$ and a line i obtained by an execution of (3.1) above such that

$$\mathcal{V} = \mathsf{Line}_i(Q, \mathcal{I}, \mathcal{V}').$$

$\square$

With these properties, we are now ready to make precise the notion of *implementation*, to define the circumstances in which a given query plan *correctly implements* a given user query.

Definition 3.8   (User Query Implementation)   Let S denote an FOL signature. An interpretation $\mathcal{I}$ of S is a *plan interpretation* if, for any atomic query plan Q' induced by S, Q' is terminating, sound and complete relative to $\mathcal{I}$.

Let Σ denote a theory over S and ϕ a well-formed formula in WFF(S). Then ϕ is a *logical consequence of Σ for plan interpretations*, written

$$\Sigma \models_p \phi \,,$$

if and only if, for any plan interpretation $\mathcal{I}$ of S and valuation $\mathcal{V}$ over $\mathcal{I}$, if $\mathcal{I}, \mathcal{V} \models \psi$ for every $\psi \in \Sigma$, then $\mathcal{I}, \mathcal{V} \models \phi$.

Let Q' denote a query plan in PLAN(S) and Q a user query in WWF(S) for which $\mathsf{Fv}(\mathsf{Uq}(Q')) = \mathsf{Fv}(Q)$ and $\mathsf{Param}(\mathsf{Uq}(Q')) = \mathsf{Param}(Q)$. Then Q' *implements* Q *in theory* Σ, written

$$\Sigma \models Q \lhd Q' \,,$$

if and only if the following conditions are satisfied:

1. Q' is terminating, sound and complete relative to any plan interpretation $\mathcal{I}$;

2. Q' produces a set relative to any plan interpretation $\mathcal{I}$ and valuation $\mathcal{V}$ over $\mathcal{I}$; and

3. $\Sigma \models_p \forall x_1, \dots, x_n.(Q \equiv \mathsf{Uq}(Q'))$, where $\mathsf{Fv}(Q) = \{x_1, \dots, x_n\}$.

$\square$

Observe that the atomic query plans in the previous section are all terminating, sound and complete for any plan interpretation by assumption. Thus, for the physical design of ACME's PAYROLL system

Σ relating to either OPTION 1 or OPTION 3 for its logical design, and for any of the atomic query plans $Q' = $ "$\texttt{emp-array}i(z, x, y)$",

$$\emptyset \models \mathsf{Uq}(Q') \lhd Q'$$

will hold by assumption, the plan *always* implements its user query mapping in theory Σ. The conclusion that these plans implement respective user queries will then be a logical consequence of Σ if it contains enough correspondence constraints that relate the logical and physical signatures of PAYROLL. (An example for such constraints was outlined in Example 3.2 of the previous section on file scans.)

3.3 CONJUNCTIVE PLANS

We now add a number of operators to our plan language, enough to express *conjunctive query plans* that are analogs of the class of (user) conjunctive queries. In textbook presentations of the relational algebra, this will mean, roughly, adding operators that enable *renaming*, *selection*, *projection* and *natural join*. Our "attention to iterative semantics", however, enables plans that use these operators to capture a much finer level of algorithmic detail, to account for so-called *bag* or *multiset semantics*, *nested loop iteration*, *cuts*, and so on.

We start with a formal definition of our extended plan language and proceed to illustrate how the additional operators can be used to express the user PAYROLL queries introduced in Section 3.1.

Definition 3.9 (Conjunctive Query Plans) Let S denote an FOL signature. The *conjunctive query plans* induced by S add five additional productions to the grammar given by Definition 3.3 of PLAN(S).

- $Q \quad ::= \quad (Q_1 \wedge Q_2) \mid \exists x \,.\, Q \text{ (where } x \in \mathsf{V}) \mid \{Q\} \mid [Q]_i \mid \;!_i$

The productions denote additional operations in our plan language. We refer to these operations as *nested loop join*, *duplicate preserving projection*, *duplicate elimination*, *cut introduction* and *named cut*, respectively.

The definitions of *input variables*, *output variables* and *user query mapping* are extended to apply to conjunctive query plans as follows, where $\mathsf{Param}(\mathsf{Uq}(Q)) = \mathsf{In}(Q)$ always holds in the latter case:

$$\mathsf{In}(Q) \;=\; \begin{cases} \mathsf{In}(Q_1) \cup (\mathsf{In}(Q_2) - \mathsf{Out}(Q_1)) & \text{if } Q = \text{``}(Q_1 \wedge Q_2)\text{''}, \\ \mathsf{In}(Q_1) & \text{if } Q = \text{``}\exists x.Q_1\text{''}, \text{``}\{Q_1\}\text{''}, \text{ or ``}[Q_1]_i\text{''}, \text{ and} \\ \emptyset & \text{if } Q = \text{``}\;!_i\;\text{''}. \end{cases}$$

$$\mathsf{Out}(Q) \;=\; \begin{cases} \mathsf{Out}(Q_1) \cup \mathsf{Out}(Q_2) & \text{if } Q = \text{``}(Q_1 \wedge Q_2)\text{''},\\[4pt] \mathsf{Out}(Q_1) \setminus \{x\} & \text{if } Q = \text{``}\exists x.Q_1\text{''},\\[4pt] \mathsf{Out}(Q_1) & \text{if } Q = \text{``}\{Q_1\}\text{''} \text{ or ``}[Q_1]_i\text{''}, \text{ and}\\[4pt] \emptyset & \text{if } Q = \text{`` }!_i\text{ ''}. \end{cases}$$

$$\mathsf{Uq}(Q) \;=\; \begin{cases} (\mathsf{Uq}(Q_1) \wedge \mathsf{Uq}(Q_2)) & \text{if } Q = \text{``}(Q_1 \wedge Q_2)\text{''},\\[4pt] \exists x.\,\mathsf{Uq}(Q_1) & \text{if } Q = \text{``}\exists x.Q_1\text{''},\\[4pt] \mathsf{Uq}(Q_1) & \text{if } Q = \text{``}\{Q_1\}\text{''} \text{ or ``}[Q_1]_i\text{''}, \text{ and}\\[4pt] \text{true} & \text{if } Q = \text{`` }!_i\text{ ''}. \end{cases}$$

Finally, we assume any conjunctive query plan Q also satisfies two conditions:

- If $Q = \text{``}(Q_1 \wedge Q_2)\text{''}$ then $(\mathsf{Out}(Q_1) \cap \mathsf{Out}(Q_2)) = \emptyset$; and

- If $Q = \text{``}\exists x.Q_1\text{''}$ then $x \notin \mathsf{In}(Q_1)$.

$\square$

Pseudo-code for these operators that adheres to our `first/next` protocol is given in Figures 3.1 and 3.2. Our examples of query plans using these operators also assume that a given physical signature includes two additional access paths that will enable plans that compare and assign variables:

$$\{\texttt{compare}/2/2,\ \texttt{assign}/2/1\} \subseteq \mathsf{S_A},$$

that is, the binary predicates `compare` and `assign`, where $\mathsf{Bp}(\texttt{compare}) = 2$ and $\mathsf{Bp}(\texttt{assign}) = 1$. The pseudo-code for these operators is given in Figure 3.3. To ensure that these access paths behave as expected with respect to equality we assume for the remainder of the book that any theory Σ defining the constraints for a database includes the sentence

$$\forall x, y.((x \approx y) \equiv \texttt{compare}(x, y))$$

and the sentence

$$\forall x, y.((x \approx y) \equiv \texttt{assign}(x, y)) .$$

Some examples of query plans that use these operators now follow, beginning with the second and third PAYROLL queries given in Section 3.1 that were used to introduce atomic query plans that correspond to using an index. Recall that the plans were based on a very simple physical design of ACME's PAYROLL system involving an ordered array `emp-array`. However, we now assume that the array is unordered and that the only access path relating to the array is `emp-array0` which provides only the ability to "file scan" all array entries.

```
function (Q₁ ∧ Q₂)-first          function (Q₁ ∧ Q₂)-next
   if not Q₁-first return false       if Q₂-next return true
   while not Q₂-first do              while Q₁-next do
      if not Q₁-next return false        if Q₂-first return true
   return true                       return false


function (∃x.Q₁)-first            function (∃x.Q₁)-next
   return Q₁-first                   return Q₁-next


function {Q₁}-first               function {Q₁}-next
   if Q₁-first                       while Q₁-next do
```
create temporary store S   if not ⟨x₁, . . . , xₙ⟩ ∈ S
add ⟨x₁, . . . , xₙ⟩ to S   *add ⟨x₁, . . . , xₙ⟩ to S*
```
      return true                       return true
   return false
```
delete temporary store S
```
                                     return false
```

Figure 3.1: Nested loop join "$Q_1 \wedge Q_2$", duplicate preserving projection "$\exists x . Q_1$", and duplicate elimination "$\{Q_1\}$", where $\text{Out}(Q_1) = \{x_1, \ldots, x_n\}$.

Example 3.10   (Scanning and selection)   Consider the second example of a user query from Section 3.1:

> *Report the* employee-number *x and* name *y of each* employee *that has a given* salary *z.*

With our new operators, a query plan that uses access path emp-array0 to implement this query can now be formulated as follows:

$$\exists u.(\text{emp-array0}(u, x, y) \wedge \text{compare}(z, u)).$$

According to our definitions, the input and output variables of this plan are $\{z\}$ and $\{x, y\}$, respectively. An execution of this plan would proceed as follows.

1. Use access path emp-array0 to scan emp-array (an atomic query subplan).

2. For each element of emp-array returned by this scan, compare the salary field with the supplied parameter value z (by using an operator for nested cross product coupled with another atomic query subplan using access path compare).

3. If this comparison evaluates to true then add the contents of this element to the result.

```
function ([Q₁]ᵢ)-first              function ([Q₁]ᵢ)-next
    cuti := false                        if cuti return false
    return Q₁-first                      return Q₁-next


function (!ᵢ)-first                  function (!ᵢ)-next
    cuti := true                         return false
    return true
```

Figure 3.2: Cut introduction "$[Q_1]_i$" and named cut "$!_i$".

Observe that the duplicate preserving projection operation is essentially a noop in terms of its effect on execution. Also observe that duplicate elimination is not required in this case because of the logical constraint that employees have unique employee numbers.   □

```
function compare-first              function compare-next
    if x₁ = x₂ return true               return false
    return false


function assign-first               function assign-next
    x₂ := x₁                             return false
    return true
```

Figure 3.3: Comparison "$compare(x_1, x_2)$" and assignment "$assign(x_1, x_2)$."

Example 3.11   (Scanning and cutting)   Consider the third example of a user query from Section 3.1:

> *Report the* name *y of any* employee *that has a given* salary *z and* employee-number *x*.

A query plan that uses access path emp-array0 to implement this query can now be formulated as follows:

$$\exists u, v.(\text{emp-array0}(u, v, y) \wedge \text{compare}(x, v) \wedge \text{compare}(z, u)).$$

An execution of this plan would proceed by an exhaustive scan of all elements of emp-array. However, again because of the logical constraint that employees have unique employee numbers, a more efficient plan can be derived from this plan that uses the cut introduction and named cut operators to effectively terminate the scan after finding the first element in `emp-array` that matches a given value for the employee number:

$$\exists u, v.([\text{emp-array0}(u, v, y)]_1 \wedge \text{compare}(x, v) \wedge !_1 \wedge \text{compare}(z, u)).$$

$\square$

Example 3.12 (Scanning and projection)   Our final example of a conjunctive query plan illustrates when it becomes necessary to use duplicate elimination. In particular, consider a requirement to provide a list of distinct salaries for employees.

Find integers z that occur as the salary value for some `employee`.

This is formally captured by the user query:

$$\exists x, y.\text{employee}(x, y, z).$$

A plan that implements this user query is given as follows:

$$\{\exists x, y.\text{emp-array0}(z, x, y)\}.$$

The plan employs a top-level duplicate elimination operation that will use temporary store to accumulate new salary values as they occur in a scan of `emp-array` with access path `emp-array0` (see the pseudo-code for duplicate elimination in Figure 3.1). $\square$

3.4   GENERAL QUERY PLANS

The general space of first order query plans is obtained by adding two final productions to our plan language. The first introduces an operator that expresses the idea of concatenating the results of two argument query plans, thus obtaining an analogue to the class of (user) positive queries. The second introduces a "negation by failure" operator that we call *simple complement*. In textbook presentations of the relational algebra, the operators correspond, roughly, to *union* and *relative complement* or *set difference*, and by adding these operators we obtain a plan language with an expressiveness that is commonly termed *relationally complete*.

Definition 3.13 (General Query Plans)   Let S denote an FOL signature. The *query plans* induced by S add two additional productions to the grammar given by Definition 3.9 of PLAN(S).

- Q ::= $(Q_1 \vee Q_2)$ | $\neg Q$

```
function (Q₁ ∨ Q₂)-first              function (Q₁ ∨ Q₂)-next
   (Q₁ ∨ Q₂)-flag := true                if (Q₁ ∨ Q₂)-flag
   if Q₁-first return true                   if Q₁-next return true
   (Q₁ ∨ Q₂)-flag := false               (Q₁ ∨ Q₂)-flag := false
   return Q₂-first                       return Q₂-next

function (¬Q₁)-first                   function (¬Q₁)-next
   if Q₁-first return false               return false
   return true
```

Figure 3.4: Concatenation "$Q_1 \vee Q_2$" and simple complement "$\neg Q_1$".

The productions denote the final two operations in our plan language. We refer to these operations as *concatenation* and *simple complement*, respectively.

The definitions of *input variables*, *output variables* and *user query mapping* are extended to apply to query plans as follows, where, again, $\text{Param}(\text{Uq}(Q)) = \text{In}(Q)$ always holds in the latter case.

$$
\text{In}(Q) = \begin{cases} \text{In}(Q_1) \cup \text{In}(Q_2) & \text{if } Q = \text{``}(Q_1 \vee Q_2)\text{''}, \text{ and} \\ \text{In}(Q_1) & \text{if } Q = \text{``}\neg \, Q_1\text{''}. \end{cases}
$$

$$
\text{Out}(Q) = \begin{cases} \text{Out}(Q_1) \cap \text{Out}(Q_2) & \text{if } Q = \text{``}(Q_1 \vee Q_2)\text{''}, \text{ and} \\ \emptyset & \text{if } Q = \text{``}\neg \, Q_1\text{''}. \end{cases}
$$

$$
\text{Uq}(Q) = \begin{cases} (\text{Uq}(Q_1) \vee \text{Uq}(Q_2)) & \text{if } Q = \text{``}(Q_1 \vee Q_2)\text{''}, \text{ and} \\ \neg \, \text{Uq}(Q_1) & \text{if } Q = \text{``}\neg \, Q_1\text{''}. \end{cases}
$$

Finally, we assume any query plan Q satisfies two further conditions:

- If $Q = \text{``}(Q_1 \vee Q_2)\text{''}$ then $\text{Out}(Q_1) = \text{Out}(Q_2)$; and

- If $Q = \text{``}\neg \, Q_1\text{''}$ then $\text{Out}(Q_1) = \emptyset$.

□

To illustrate the use of these operators, we return to examples of user queries in Chapter 2 that were formulated to capture various hypothetical information access requirements for ACME's PAYROLL system.

Example 3.14 (Concatenation) Consider Example 2.9 in Chapter 2 in which user queries for various logical designs for PAYROLL were presented that formalized the following information request:

Find the `employee-number` *x for any* `employee` *that has a* `salary` *matching either the parameter p_1 or the parameter p_2.*

Access path `emp-array0` can be used in combination with the concatenation operator to obtain a query plan implementation as follows:

$$
\begin{aligned}
\{(\\
\quad \exists y, z.(\texttt{emp-array0}(z, x, y) \wedge \texttt{compare}(p_1, z)) \\
\quad \vee\ \exists u, v.(\texttt{emp-array0}(v, x, u) \wedge \texttt{compare}(p_2, v))) \\
\}.
\end{aligned}
$$

When executed, the plan begins by scanning `emp-array` and returning the employee number of any employee with a salary given by input parameter p_1. The plan then proceeds by scanning `emp-array` for a second time and returning the employee number of any employee with a salary given by input parameter p_2.

Observe that the user query mapping of the plan is what we have called a *positive query* in Chapter 2 since it uses concatenation as a (near) top-level operator with argument sub-plans that are conjunctive. An alternative plan can be formulated in our plan language, however, that avoids the need for two scans of `emp-array`:

$$\{\exists y, z.(\texttt{emp-array0}(z, x, y) \wedge (\texttt{compare}(p_1, z) \vee \texttt{compare}(p_2, z)))\}.$$

Indeed, this plan illustrates a common plan idiom for determining if a given value occurs in a given small fixed set of values.

The need for the duplicate elimination operator in each of the above query plans stems from two possible reasons: 1) individual employee numbers may be related to more than one salary or employee name; and 2) parameters p_1 and p_2 may not be distinct. The first possibility is ruled out by virtue of the logical design of `payroll` relating to identification and property functionality constraints, in particular, that ensure employee numbers *functionally determine* names and salaries of employees. The second possibility can be ruled out by modifying the plan to ensure the second subplan for the concatenation operator will only return additional results when p_1 and p_2 are distinct:

$$
\begin{aligned}
\exists y, z.(\texttt{emp-array0}(z, x, y) \\
\quad \wedge (\texttt{compare}(p_1, z) \vee (\neg\, \texttt{compare}(p_1, p_2) \wedge \texttt{compare}(p_2, z)))).
\end{aligned}
$$

However, note that the query mapping for this plan is no longer a positive query. An alternative formulation that avoids the introduction of a simple compliment operator by using a cut is as follows:

$$\exists y, z.(\texttt{emp-array0}(z, x, y) \wedge [(\texttt{compare}(p_1, z) \vee \texttt{compare}(p_2, z))]_1 \wedge\ !_1)).$$

□

Example 3.15   (Simple complement)   Finally, consider Example 2.10 in Chapter 2 in which user queries were presented that formalized:

Find the `employee-number` *x for any* `employee` *that has a* `name` *that is also unique.*

Access path `emp-array0` can now be used in combination with the simple complement operator to obtain an implementation:

$$\exists y, z.(\text{emp-array0}(z, x, y)$$
$$\wedge \neg \exists u, v, w.(\text{emp-array0}(u, v, w) \wedge \text{compare}(y, w) \wedge \neg \text{compare}(x, v))).$$

The inner query plan within the scope of the first simple complement operator serves as a filter on possible employee numbers that are scanned in an outer loop of `emp-array`.

One might suspect that the performance of this plan can be improved somewhat by using a cut operator after the second invocation of `compare` in the inner query plan:

$$\exists y, z.(\text{emp-array0}(z, x, y)$$
$$\wedge \neg \exists u, v, w.([\text{emp-array0}(u, v, w)]_1 \wedge \text{compare}(y, w) \wedge \neg \text{compare}(x, v)) \wedge \ !_1).$$

However, a more careful trace of Q-first and Q-next calls relating to our simple complement operator will reveal that both plans have identical behavior (notwithstanding the overhead for maintaining variable `cut1` in the latter case).   □

We now list a number of properties that are satisfied by query plans expressed in terms of our plan language. Proving that the properties are true is straightforward and is left as an exercise for the reader. (Most will require reasoning by induction on the size of the query plan. The remainder are almost immediate consequences of our definitions.)

Theorem 3.16   Let S denote an FOL signature. Then the following properties hold for any query plan $Q \in$ PLAN(S).

(with respect to plan properties)

1. Q is terminating for any plan interpretation $\mathcal{I}$ of S.

2. If Q has the form "$(Q_1 \wedge Q_2)$", "$\exists x.Q_1$", "$\{Q_1\}$", "$(Q_1 \vee Q_2)$" or " $\neg Q_1$", and if Q_i is sound and complete for any plan interpretation $\mathcal{I}$ of S, for all i, then so is Q.

3. If Q has the form "$(Q_1 \wedge Q_2)$" or "$[Q_1]_i$", and if Q_1 and Q_2 produce sets relative to any plan interpretation $\mathcal{I}$ of S and any valuation $\mathcal{V}$ over $\mathcal{I}$, then so does Q.

4. If Q has the form "$\{Q_1\}$", "$!_i$" or "$\neg Q_1$", then Q produces a set relative to any plan interpretation $\mathcal{I}$ of S and any valuation $\mathcal{V}$ over $\mathcal{I}$.

5. If Q is terminating, sound and complete for any plan interpretation $\mathcal{I}$ of S, then

$$\emptyset \models \mathsf{Uq}(Q) \lhd \{Q\} \, .$$

(with respect to join order)

1. If Q has the form "$((Q_1 \wedge Q_2) \wedge Q_3)$", then, for any plan interpretation $\mathcal{I}$ of S and any valuation $\mathcal{V}$ over $\mathcal{I}$,

$$\mathsf{Size}(Q, \mathcal{I}, \mathcal{V}) = \mathsf{Size}((Q_1 \wedge (Q_2 \wedge Q_3)), \mathcal{I}, \mathcal{V})$$

and

$$\mathsf{Line}_i(Q, \mathcal{I}, \mathcal{V}) = \mathsf{Line}_i((Q_1 \wedge (Q_2 \wedge Q_3)), \mathcal{I}, \mathcal{V})$$

for $1 \leq i \leq \mathsf{Size}(Q, \mathcal{I}, \mathcal{V})$.

2. If Q has the form "$(Q_1 \wedge Q_2)$" and $(\mathsf{Out}(Q_1) \cap \mathsf{In}(Q_2)) = \emptyset$, then, for any plan interpretation $\mathcal{I}$ of S and any valuation $\mathcal{V}$ over $\mathcal{I}$,

$$\mathsf{Size}(Q, \mathcal{I}, \mathcal{V}) = \mathsf{Size}((Q_2 \wedge Q_1), \mathcal{I}, \mathcal{V})$$

and

$$\mathsf{Exec}(Q, \mathcal{I}, \mathcal{V}) = \mathsf{Exec}((Q_2 \wedge Q_1), \mathcal{I}, \mathcal{V}).$$

$\square$

3.5 SUMMARY

Our language for query plans consists of eight operators. One of the operators, the first that we introduced, allows us to formulate *atomic* query plans. This entailed a small revision to FOL signatures in which we introduced the notion of an *access path* P, a predicate symbol with a *binding pattern* that represents a material capability to access the interpretation of P. We also introduced two particular access paths, `compare` and `assign`, that provide a material capability to compare and assign elements of a domain according to the semantics of equality. In practical terms, this amounts to an assumption that copying or comparing finite length strings, "ints", "reals" and so on, is always possible.

Duplicate elimination is our only operator that requires storing an arbitrarily sized result. In particular, we have avoided introducing a more general assignment operator for creating temporary access paths that might be used in other parts of a query plan. This would be useful in cases where a plan has common subexpressions that compute the same set of n-tuples. A more general assignment operator, however, leads inexorably to the general problem of automated physical design, a topic that is beyond the scope of this book. However, note that the database notion of a *materialized view* is easily accommodated in our framework (see Exercise 3.9 below).

We have also avoided introducing a sort operator since this would require us to considerably complicate the execution semantics for query plans. Indeed, this requires at least the effort needed to enable user queries to express ordering and ranking criteria, which is also beyond the scope of this book. However, the need to consider a sorting operator for performance reasons, e.g., to express so-called "merge joins", is not so clear cut; see our topics for discussion in the next chapter.

Often, there are many query plans that implement a given user query that can vary fundamentally in their execution complexity, measured in terms of the size of an interpretation of the access paths, or, more practically, in their performance on typical workloads. Both complexity analysis in the former case and cost estimation based on statistical knowledge in the latter case are also beyond the scope of this book. Note that, to the best of our knowledge, cost estimation is considered extra-logically in the literature.

3.6   BIBLIOGRAPHIC NOTES

Codd [1972] proposed a collection of operations for his relational model that he called the *relational algebra*, although he saw this language as an option for expressing user queries. The operations mapped finite sets of tuples to a set of tuples. He also showed how this language is equivalent to a syntactic subset of well-formed formulae in FOL in which variables satisfy a *range restriction* (see Exercise 3.6).

Our iterated semantics for query plans is called a *bag semantics* or *multiset semantics* in the literature. Early work by Chaudhuri and Vardi [1993] on a bag semantics for queries considers the problem of determining if the results of a conjunctive query were necessarily a "sub-bag" of another conjunctive query.

Ullman [1985] introduced binding patterns in the form of a *predicate adornment* for predicate symbols: a symbol of arity k is combined with a sequence of k "b"s and "f"s to indicate a mode of use of the symbol in query evaluation. More recently, Avron [2008] considers how query plans developed in this chapter compare to notions of *absoluteness* and *constructibility* in set theory and formal arithmetic. The comparison assumes a set semantics for query plans in which duplicate elimination is always performed as a final operation in a query plan.

There has not been much work on developing a semantics beyond a bag semantics that accounts for ordering the results of user queries or that is implicit in an access path. One exception is the *possible results semantics* for user queries and query plans in which possible results were defined in terms of a list theory [Coburn and Weddell, 1993]. Reasoning about "order by" clauses in SQL in the context of query compilation has been considered extra-logically [Simmen et al., 1996]. Also, constraints that express ordering conditions among the attributes of a relation have also been considered [Ginsburg and Hull, 1983]. Such constraints can express, for example, that an employee's salary is never less than another employee's salary when the other employee is younger.

3.7   EXERCISES WITH TOPICS FOR DISCUSSION

Exercise 3.1   Show how logical design can be an issue in physical design. In particular, show how it might be appropriate to introduce predicate symbols in a physical vocabulary that are not access paths. (Hint: lots of ideas for when this is necessary are suggested in the next chapter.)

Exercise 3.2   Our execution semantics for query plans is essentially single threaded. Consider how one might introduce alternatives to our nested loop join and concatenation operators that would enable one to express concurrent or parallel query evaluation.

Exercise 3.3   One can relax our requirement that pseudo-code (3.1) in Section 3.2 terminates by requiring instead that each line must be produced in a finite amount of time. A query plan that has this behavior is called a *streaming query* in the literature. Explore how streaming queries can be accommodated in our framework, in particular, how access paths and query plans need to be modified to ensure that each line produced by running (3.1) will indeed be printed after a finite amount of time has elapsed.

Exercise 3.4   Our assumptions about the exact behavior of an access path during execution is quite open-ended. Show how one can introduce access paths in a physical design that function as locks. In particular, show how deadlock free tree protocols for lock based concurrency control can be captured as part of physical design.

Exercise 3.5   Given an interpretation $\mathcal{I}_1$, an n-tuple t is a *certain answer* to a user query Q if t occurs in the evaluation of Q with respect to $\mathcal{I}_1$ and if, for any interpretation $\mathcal{I}_2$ that agrees with $\mathcal{I}_1$ on its interpretation of all access paths, t also occurs in the evaluation of Q with respect to $\mathcal{I}_2$. Is the set of all certain answers for a user query always defined? Can all certain answers to a user query be computed by some query plan in our plan language when the binding pattern for all access paths is zero? (Hint: consider transitive closure.) Explore cases in which computing all certain answers for conjunctive or positive user queries might be useful. Explore the utility of computing all certain answers for user queries that mention negation.

Exercise 3.6   Show how Codd's relational algebra maps to query plans in our framework. Hint: assume any predicate symbol P/n in a given signature S is also an access path $P/n/0$.

Exercise 3.7   Show how first-order definable queries in SQL also map to query plans in our framework.

Exercise 3.8   Prove Theorem 3.16.

Exercise 3.9   In work on databases, a *view definition* corresponds to a constraint of the form

$$\forall x_1, \ldots, x_n.(P(x_1, \ldots, x_n) \equiv Q)$$

over a logical signature, where Q is a user query with free variables $\{x_1, \ldots, x_n\}$ and with no parameters, and where P is a n-ary predicate symbol called the *view name*. If the view name P is also an access path, then P is also called a *materialized view*. Explore how databases impose additional syntactic conditions on a user query Q that is used to define a view, and on how databases support additional access paths derived from a materialized view P.

CHAPTER 4

On Practical Physical Design

We now consider how our plan language together with basic data structures can be composed in various ways to capture more sophisticated data structures and physical design artifacts that are commonly deployed with relational database technology. We investigate how pointers, hashing, user-defined functions, two-level store, and so on, can be accommodated without any need to introduce additional plan operators. Thus, one obtains a practical physical design by:

1. adding new predicate symbols and access paths, and

2. adding new constraints

to the signature and to the theory of a logical design. We illustrate the approach using an extension of the OPTION 1 design for ACME's PAYROLL system introduced and used in Chapters 2 and 3. This extended design adds two additional predicate symbols to the logical signature S_L of PAYROLL to accommodate information about how employees relate to departments.

OPTION 1 (*extended*).

- $S_L^P = \{\texttt{employee}/3, \texttt{department}/3, \texttt{works}/2\}$, and
- $S_L^F = \emptyset$.

The intention for the `employee` predicate remains unchanged from Chapter 2: position 1 of the predicate corresponds to `employee-number` values of employees, and so on. Predicate `department` associates a department `name` and `manager`, positions 2 and 3 of the predicate, with a unique `number` for the department. Note that the values for position 3 will correspond to the `employee-number` for some employee. The third `works` predicate associates the number of an employee with the number of a department, positions 1 and 2, respectively. The predicate holds when the corresponding employee works for the corresponding department.

Figure 4.1 summarizes the extended logical design. Predicates correspond to boxes in the figure, with the role of predicate positions indicated by keywords. Note that positions serving the role of visible object identifiers (usually called *primary keys*) are listed first and distinguished from the remaining positions by a horizontal line. The figure also includes a number of directed edges. These correspond to TGDs that "point to" or "reference" the position of predicates that correspond to primary keys (usually called *foreign keys*). All this is formally captured by the following collection of logical constraints over S_L:

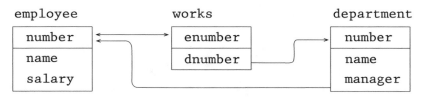

Figure 4.1: Logical schema diagram.

I1. Employees can be identified by their employee number (from Chapter 2):

$$\forall x_1, x_2, y_1, y_2.(\exists z.(\texttt{employee}(z, x_1, x_2) \land \texttt{employee}(z, y_1, y_2))$$
$$\to ((x_1 \approx y_1) \land (x_2 \approx y_2))).$$

I2. Departments can also be identified by their department number:

$$\forall x_1, x_2, y_1, y_2.(\exists z.(\texttt{department}(z, x_1, x_2) \land \texttt{department}(z, y_1, y_2))$$
$$\to ((x_1 \approx y_1) \land (x_2 \approx y_2))).$$

I3. At most one working relationship to a department can exist for a given employee:

$$\forall x, y.(\exists z.(\texttt{works}(z, x) \land \texttt{works}(z, y)) \to (x \approx y)).$$

I4. Only employees can be the manager of a department:

$$\forall x.(\exists y, z.\texttt{department}(y, z, x) \to \exists u, v.\texttt{employee}(x, u, v)).$$

I5. Working relationships can only exists between employees and departments:

$$\forall x, y.(\texttt{works}(x, y)$$
$$\to \exists u_1, u_2, v_1, v_2.(\texttt{employee}(x, u_1, v_1) \land \texttt{department}(y, u_2, v_2))).$$

I6. Every employee must work:

$$\forall x.(\exists y, z.\texttt{employee}(x, y, z) \to \exists u.\texttt{works}(x, u)).$$

The first three constraints are EGDs relating to identification. The remaining three constraints are TGDs that correspond to the foreign keys in Figure 4.1.

Note that the summary effect of constraints *I3*, *I5* and *I6* is to ensure that predicate `works` encodes a total function that maps employees to departments. An analogous effect is achieved in a different way in (logically) encoding the manager of a department by adding position 3 to predicate `department` together with the "typing" constraint *I4*. We have done this on purpose to illustrate the flexibility of logical design, and, later on, to show that exercising such options do not (necessarily) impact physical design.

4.1   REFERENCES, POINTERS AND LINKED STRUCTURES

One of the most powerful idioms of physical design relies on the assumption that some underlying data store is based on the RAM model. As a consequence, access to records that are located in such store can be accomplished in constant time when search keys correspond to pointer values that *address* or *reference* the store. Indeed, dereferencing a pointer value is the ultimate means of data access in the RAM model. Note that this idiom applies not only to main memory data but also to data stored on external devices that provide close to random access, such as magnetic discs (we explore "magnetic disk RAM" in more detail in Section 4.4).

Our approach to modeling this idiom is as follows: we assume that data is organized in *records* of the form

```
record r of
   field-type₁ f₁
       ⋮
   field-typeₖ fₖ
```

located at a particular *address* in the RAM storage. The types of the fields of such records can be atomic values, such as integers and strings (we have already assumed these are present in our current physical model) and, in fields typed as a *reference* or as a *pointer*, values called *addresses* that encode the locations of records in the RAM storage. We model this by a collection of access paths:

$$r\text{-}f_1/2/1, \ldots, r\text{-}f_k/2/1.$$

The intended meaning of an atomic query plan $r\text{-}f_i(x_1, x_2)$ is to interpret the binding for variable x_1 as an address of an "r" record. When executed, RAM storage is accessed using this address to retrieve the value of field f_i into variable x_2. With respect to our `first/next` protocol, pseudocode that reflects this intended meaning is given as follows:

```
function r-fᵢ-first            function r-fᵢ-next
   x₂ := x₁ -> fᵢ                  return false.
   return true
```

We also assume that each of the access paths is associated with a constraint that ensures the operation of extracting a field from a record is a function:

$$\forall x, y_1, y_2.((r\text{-}f_i(x, y_1) \wedge r\text{-}f_i(x, y_2)) \rightarrow (y_1 \approx y_2)).$$

Indeed, this constraint is reflected in the pseudocode's `next` function by virtue of an immediate return of `false`.

Example 4.1   (A physical design for PAYROLL **with references)**   Recall the latest logical design of `payroll` given by OPTION 1. One way to encode data for this design is to represent individual `employee` and `department` entities as records conforming to the following `emp` and `dept` declarations:

```
record emp of                    record dept of
      integer   num                    integer   num
      string    name                   string    name
      integer   salary                 reference manager
      reference dept
```

and then to organize the records in two separate collection data structures (such as arrays or linked lists) called `empfile` and `deptfile`. These data structures allow us to scan the addresses of all `emp` and `dept` records that represent `employee` and `department` entities. A physical design for this data encoding is given as follows:

Physical Signature:

$$S_A = \{ \quad \texttt{empfile}/1/0, \texttt{depfile}/1/0,$$
$$\texttt{emp-num}/2/1, \texttt{emp-name}/2/1, \texttt{emp-salary}/2/1, \texttt{emp-dept}/2/1,$$
$$\texttt{dept-num}/2/1, \texttt{dept-name}/2/1, \texttt{dept-manager}/2/1 \qquad \},$$

Physical Constraints Σ' (a selection):

$p1$. *Every* emp *record has all its fields*:

(a) $\forall x.(\texttt{empfile}(x) \rightarrow \exists y.\texttt{emp-num}(x, y))$,

(b) $\forall x.(\texttt{empfile}(x) \rightarrow \exists y.\texttt{emp-name}(x, y))$,

(c) $\forall x.(\texttt{empfile}(x) \rightarrow \exists y.\texttt{emp-salary}(x, y))$, and

(d) $\forall x.(\texttt{empfile}(x) \rightarrow \exists y.\texttt{emp-dept}(x, y))$.

$p2$. *The range of* emp-dept *is a* dept *record in* deptfile:

$\forall x, y.(\texttt{emp-dept}(x, y) \rightarrow \texttt{deptfile}(y))$.

$p3$. *Every* dept *record has all its fields*:

(a) $\forall x.(\texttt{deptfile}(x) \rightarrow \exists y.\texttt{dept-num}(x, y))$,

(b) $\forall x.(\texttt{deptfile}(x) \rightarrow \exists y.\texttt{dept-name}(x, y))$ and

(c) $\forall x.(\texttt{deptfile}(x) \rightarrow \exists y.\texttt{dept-manager}(x, y))$.

$p4$. *The range of* dept-manager *is an* emp *record in* empfile:

$\forall x, y.(\texttt{dept-manager}(x, y) \rightarrow \texttt{empfile}(y))$

Mapping Constraints Σ'' (a selection):

$m1$. *For every* employee *there is an* emp *record*:

$\forall x.y, z.(\texttt{employee}(x, y, z) \rightarrow \exists w.(\texttt{empfile}(w) \wedge \texttt{emp-num}(w, x)))$.

*m*2. *The contents of the* name *field of an* emp *record corresponding to a particular* employee *contains this employee's name*:

$$\forall x, y, z, w.((\text{employee}(x, y, z) \wedge \text{emp-num}(w, x))$$
$$\rightarrow \text{emp-name}(w, y)).$$

*m*3. *Same for the* salary *field*:

$$\forall x, y, z, w.((\text{employee}(x, y, z) \wedge \text{emp-num}(w, x))$$
$$\rightarrow \text{emp-salary}(w, z)).$$

*m*4. *The contents of the* dept *field of an* emp *record is a reference to the* dept *record that represents the* department *for which this employee* works:

$$\forall x, y, z, w, u.((\text{employee}(x, y, z) \wedge \text{emp-num}(w, x) \wedge \text{works}(x, u)$$
$$\wedge \text{dept-num}(v, u)) \rightarrow \text{emp-dept}(w, v)).$$

*m*5. *Every* emp *record in* empfile *represents an* employee:

$$\forall x, y, z, w.((\text{empfile}(w) \wedge \text{emp-num}(w, x) \wedge \text{emp-name}(w, y)$$
$$\wedge \text{emp-salary}(w, z)) \rightarrow \text{employee}(x, y, z)).$$

*m*6. *Every* emp *record and the associated* dept *record referenced by the* dept *field represents a* works *relationship*:

$$\forall x, y, v, w.((\text{empfile}(w) \wedge \text{emp-num}(w, x) \wedge \text{emp-dept}(w, v)$$
$$\wedge \text{dept-num}(v, y)) \rightarrow \text{works}(x, y)).$$

*m*7. *For every* department *there is a* dept *record*:

$$\forall x, y, z.(\text{department}(x, y, z) \rightarrow \exists w.(\text{deptfile}(w) \wedge \text{dept-num}(w, x))).$$

*m*8. *Every* dept *record has the proper contents for its* name *field*:

$$\forall x, y, z, w.((\text{department}(x, y, z) \wedge \text{dept-num}(w, x)) \rightarrow \text{dept-name}(w, y)),$$

*m*9. *... and also for its* manager *field*:

$$\forall x, y, z, w.((\text{department}(x, y, z) \wedge \text{dept-num}(w, x))$$
$$\rightarrow \exists v.(\text{dept-manager}(w, v) \wedge \text{emp-num}(v, z))).$$

*m*10. *Every* dept *record in the* deptfile *represents a* department:

$$\forall x, y, z, w, v.((\text{dept-num}(w, x) \wedge \text{dept-name}(w, y) \wedge \text{dept-manager}(w, v)$$
$$\wedge \text{emp-num}(v, z)) \rightarrow \text{department}(x, y, z)).$$

□

Example 4.2 (Queries and their plans with field navigation)   Now consider a user query to *list employee numbers, names and department names for all employees*:

$$Q = \exists y, v, w.(\text{employee}(x_1, x_2, y) \wedge \text{works}(x_1, v) \wedge \text{department}(v, x_3, w)).$$

One plan Q' that implements this user query with respect to the above physical design is defined as follows:

$$Q' = \{\exists w, v.(\texttt{empfile}(w) \wedge \texttt{emp-num}(w, x_1) \wedge \texttt{emp-name}(w, x_2)$$
$$\wedge\ \texttt{emp-dept}(w, v) \wedge \texttt{dept-name}(v, x_3))\}.$$

Indeed, it holds that $\Sigma \models Q \lhd Q'$ (cf. Definition 3.8), where Σ consists of the above physical design for PAYROLL. In particular, the nested loops joins combined with the pseudocode for the field extraction access paths defined by this design yield the desired plan for the query: for each employee record, extract the needed fields and, to retrieve the name of the employee's manager, *follow* the reference in the dept field and then extract the value directly from a dept record. Note that, once a reference to an employee record is obtained, all remaining operations are dereferencing operations that run in $O(1)$ in the RAM model.   □

Example 4.3 (EGDs and eliminating duplicate elimination)   Consider the equality generating dependencies in the form of functional constraints in the physical design, in particular the constraint

$$\forall x, y_1, y_2.(\texttt{emp-num}(y_1, x) \wedge \texttt{emp-num}(y_1, x)) \rightarrow (y_1 \approx y_2),$$

stating that the emp records correspond *one-to-one* to employee entities (identified by their employee number), and constraints expressing the functionality of field access. Altogether, they imply that the query plan

$$Q' = \exists w, v.(\texttt{empfile}(w) \wedge \texttt{emp-num}(w, x_1) \wedge \texttt{emp-name}(w, x_2)$$
$$\wedge\ \texttt{emp-dept}(w, v) \wedge \texttt{dept-name}(v, x_3))$$

also implements the user query from Example 4.2. In this case, the final duplicate elimination operation has been omitted and one obtains a plan that runs in $O(n)$ time, where n is the number of employee entities. (Remember that the underlying data structure with emp records is an array or linked list.)   □

4.1.1   EFFICIENT SEARCH AND SECONDARY INDICES

Introducing explicit *references* to records simplifies the understanding of *secondary indexing*: a secondary index is simply a (search) data structure that stores the search keys paired with appropriate references to the records that comprise the search space.

Example 4.4 (Nested loops and secondary indices)   Consider a user query that *list pairs of employee numbers of employees with the same name*:

$$\exists y, z, w.(\texttt{employee}(x_1, y, z) \wedge \texttt{employee}(x_2, y, w)).$$

One query plan that implements this query is given as follows:

$$\exists y, z, w, v.(\texttt{empfile}(v) \wedge \texttt{emp-num}(v, x_1) \wedge \texttt{emp-name}(v, y)$$
$$\wedge\, \texttt{empfile}(w) \wedge \texttt{emp-num}(w, x_2) \wedge \texttt{emp-name}(w, z) \wedge \texttt{compare}(y, z)).$$

However, this plan is not desirable since it considers all pairs of employees and then selects those with the same name. An additional *access path* that allows us to efficiently find references to employee records given an employee *name* (such as a search tree or an ordered array; cf. Chapter 3) would enable plans for the query that avoid this. In particular, consider extending the physical design by an access path `empidx-name/2/1` (accompanied by an implementation of the search structure) and the constraint

$$\forall x, y.(\texttt{eidx-name}(x, y) \equiv (\texttt{empfile}(y) \wedge \texttt{emp-name}(y, x))).$$

An alternative plan implementing the query that avoids the need to compare all pairs of employees is now possible:

$$\exists y, w, v.(\texttt{empfile}(v)\wedge \texttt{emp-num}(v, x_1) \wedge \texttt{emp-name}(v, y)$$
$$\wedge\, \texttt{empidx-name}(y, w) \wedge \texttt{emp-num}(w, x_2)).$$

$\square$

In the above, we have *stored* references to records in the search structure. Alternatively, we could have embedded the actual `emp` records into the search structure itself. Indeed, this difference is the basis for classifying indexes as *primary* (storing actual records) and *secondary* (storing references). Allowing references to be first-class citizens in the physical design essentially erases this difference. Hence, there is no longer any need for the notion of *secondary index*: this simply becomes an access path that relates the search keys to appropriate *references* to records (stored elsewhere).

Note that while we used a *monolithic* search structure we can often refine the access path using more primitive building blocks and additional constraints (we show an example in Section 4.3).

4.2   NULLS, PARTITIONS AND RUN-TIME TYPING

4.2.1   NULLS INDICATING VALUE INAPPLICABLE

Now consider a modification to the logical design of PAYROLL given by OPTION I, namely, the removal of the second constraint:

$$\forall x, y, z.(\texttt{employee}(x, y, z) \rightarrow \exists u.\texttt{works}(x, u)).$$

This change allows for the possibility that employees are not associated with any department, a relaxed design in which each employee now works for *at most one* department. Our goal is to accommodate this change in requirements *without* the need for a major modification of the physical design: we still want employees and departments to be represented by the `emp` and `dept` records and *signal* the fact that an employee is *not* associated with a department by filling the dept field of the associated emp record with some default value different from other references, typically called NULL.

This is a common idiom in a *physical design* when we desire to model (the absence of) optional information using a default NULL value. For this purpose we introduce an additional access path, null/1/1, that implements a generic test for a NULL reference, for example, using the following pseudocode:

```
function null-first                    function null-next
    if (x₁ == NULL) return true            return false .
    return false
```

Example 4.5   (Optional data: NULL as value inapplicable)   To model this situation, we augment the physical design with an additional access path and constraints:

Physical Signature: $\{\texttt{null/1/1}\} \subseteq \mathsf{S_A}$

Constraints:

1. *The* dept *field of an* emp *record either contains a reference to a* dept *record representing a department, or a* NULL *value*:

   $\forall x, y.(\texttt{emp-dept}(x, y) \rightarrow (\texttt{deptfile}(y) \lor \texttt{null}(y)))$.

2. *References to* dept *records are distinct from the* NULL *value*:

   $\forall x.(\texttt{dept-file}(x) \rightarrow \neg\texttt{null}(x))$.

3. *There is only one* NULL *value*:

   $\forall x, y.((\texttt{null}(x) \land \texttt{null}(y)) \rightarrow (x \approx y))$.

   □

Having a simple taxonomy of *values* in this way enables one to avoid the need to state properties of the NULL value on each occasion of use.

Example 4.6   (Queries and plans that test for NULL)   Consider a user query to *list numbers and names of all employees that do not work for any department*:

$$Q = \exists y.(\texttt{employee}(x_1, x_2, y) \land \neg \exists z.\texttt{works}(x_1, z)).$$

A query plan Q' that implements this user query with respect to the modified physical design is given as follows:

$$Q' = \exists y, z.(\texttt{empfile}(y) \land \texttt{emp-num}(y, x_1) \land \texttt{emp-name}(y, x_2)$$
$$\land \texttt{emp-dept}(y, z) \land \texttt{null}(z)).$$

In particular, $\Sigma \models Q \lhd Q'$ follows straightforwardly from the fact that, under the new physical design, $\Sigma \models_p \forall x_1, \ldots, x_n.(Q \equiv \mathsf{Uq}(Q'))$, where $\mathsf{Fv}(Q) = \{x_1, \ldots, x_n\}$, and by observing that x_1 is a unique key value (cf. Section 5.2.6).

Now consider the user query from Example 4.2 to *list employee numbers, names and department names for all employees* (who must now work for a department):

$$Q = \exists y, z, w.(\texttt{employee}(x_1, x_2, y) \wedge \texttt{works}(x_1, z) \wedge \texttt{department}(z, x_3, w)).$$

A query plan Q' that implements this user query is given by:

$$Q' = \exists y, z.(\texttt{empfile}(y) \wedge \texttt{emp-num}(y, x_1) \wedge \texttt{emp-name}(y, x_2)$$
$$\wedge \texttt{emp-dept}(y, z) \wedge (\neg \texttt{null}(z)) \wedge \texttt{dept-name}(z, x_3)).$$

Indeed, the "$\neg\,\texttt{null}(x)$" literal in this plan corresponds exactly to the standard imperative programming idiom of ensuring that a pointer is not the NULL pointer prior to a dereference. □

4.2.2   HORIZONTAL PARTITIONING

A similar approach to how one can incorporate null inapplicable values in physical design can be used to achieve a seamless *horizontal partitioning* into a fixed number of partitions. We illustrate this in the following by using *numerical constants*. This is a violation of our assumption that signatures are free of constant and function symbols that is easily rectified. (In particular, see Exercise 4.2 for an approach that avoids the need for constant symbols.)

Example 4.7   (Partitioning employees by salary)   Consider the following three constraints:

$$\forall x.(\texttt{empfile-low}(x) \equiv \exists y.(\texttt{empfile}(x) \wedge \texttt{emp-sal}(x, y) \wedge (y \le 30k))),$$

$$\forall x.(\texttt{empfile-mid}(x) \equiv \exists y.(\texttt{empfile}(x) \wedge \texttt{emp-sal}(x, y) \wedge (30k < y) \wedge (y \le 130k)))$$

and

$$\forall x.(\texttt{empfile-high}(x) \equiv \exists y.(\texttt{empfile}(x) \wedge \texttt{emp-sal}(x, y) \wedge (y < 130k))).$$

The constraints partition emp records into three disjoint subsets based on the value of the sal field. For this, we assume that integer values come with (at least conceptual) predicates denoting a linear order "$\le$" and a strict linear order "$<$" interpreted in the standard way. An alternative to relying on the properties of order would be to add taxonomic constraints to the design that ensure the three partitions are disjoint and that they cover all employees.

Now consider a user query to *list employee numbers for employees making at most* 130k:

$$\exists y, z.(\texttt{employee}(x_1, y, z) \wedge (z \le 130k)).$$

Also assume the physical design for payroll is revised by "demoting" access path empfile to the status of a logical predicate and then by adding three additional access paths, one for each partition:

- $\{\texttt{empfile}/1/0\} \subseteq S_P$ and

- $\{\texttt{empfile-low}/1/0, \texttt{empfile-mid}/1/0, \texttt{empfile-high}/1/0\} \subseteq S_A$.

A plan using concatenation that implements this query is then given by:

$$\exists y.((\texttt{empfile-low}(y) \vee \texttt{empfile-mid}(y)) \wedge \texttt{emp-num}(y, x_1)).$$

An alternative plan using simple complement is possible if we "re-promote" empfile to its original status as an access path:

- $\{\texttt{empfile}/1/0\} \subseteq S_A$.

This alternative plan is given as follows:

$$\exists y.(\texttt{empfile}(y) \wedge \neg\, \texttt{empfile-high}(y) \wedge \texttt{emp-num}(y, x_1)).$$

This plan assumes that the partition covers all employee records and that constraints such as

$$\forall x.((x \leq 130k) \rightarrow (x \leq 30k))$$

can also be deduced.   □

With this latest physical design, we are not yet able to find a plan for a user query to *list employee numbers for employees making at most* 50k. This is a consequence of lacking any material way of comparing numbers, a situation we revisit in Section 4.3.

4.2.3   RUN-TIME TYPING

A common feature of object-oriented databases that support the definition of elaborate taxonomic knowledge is to support membership in a subclass to be tested at runtime when given a reference to an object in a superclass. We illustrate how this is accommodated in the following by considering a variation of Example 4.7 above to the design of PAYROLL to incorporate the logical notion of employees with high salaries.

Example 4.8   (Testing for membership in a subclass)   Assume the signature of PAYROLL is revised as follows:

- $\{\texttt{high-employee}/1\} \subseteq S_L$, and

- $\{\texttt{emp-high}/1/1\} \subseteq S_A$.

Also assume the following constraints are added to Σ.

1. *Highly paid employees are a subset of employees*:

$$\forall x.(\texttt{high-employee}(x) \rightarrow \exists y, z.\texttt{employee}(x, y, z)).$$

2. *A reference to an* emp *record for an employee is also a reference to* emp *record for a highly paid employee whenever the reference also qualifies as* emp-high:

$$\forall x, y.((\texttt{empfile}(y) \wedge \texttt{emp-high}(y) \wedge \texttt{emp-num}(y, x)) \equiv \texttt{high-employee}(x)).$$

The revision modifies the logical design of PAYROLL by adding a "subclass" of employee called high-employee, and then by introducing the access path emp-high to enable checking at runtime for membership in high-employee. For example, consider a user query to *list employee numbers for employees that are highly paid*:

$$\texttt{high-employee}(x).$$

A plan that implements this query is given as follows:

$$\exists y.(\texttt{empfile}(y) \wedge \texttt{emp-high}(y) \wedge \texttt{emp-num}(y, x)).$$

□

4.3   BUILT-IN FUNCTIONS AND HASHING

We can support the usual operations on *built-in* data types, such as *integers*, by (a) defining appropriate access paths that provide implementations for such operations, and (b) defining constraints that link these access paths with the symbols in user queries and constraints.

Access paths:

• For integers: plus/3/2, minus/3/2, less/2/2, lesseq/2/2 .

Constraints:

1. Addition on the logical level is implemented by the access paths plus and minus:

$$\forall x, y, z.((x + y = z) \equiv \texttt{plus}(x, y, z))$$
$$\forall x, y, z.((x + y = z) \equiv \texttt{minus}(z, x, y))$$
$$\forall x, y, z.((x + y = z) \equiv \texttt{minus}(z, y, x)) \,.$$

2. Order comparison is implemented by the less access path:

$$\forall x, y.((x < y) \equiv \texttt{less}(x, y))$$
$$\forall x, y.((x \leq y) \equiv \texttt{lesseq}(x, y)) \,.$$

Observe the *crucial* use of the *binding patterns*: it is not possible to define, e.g., plus/3/0 since that would violate the conditions in Definition 3.7 that require atomic query plans to terminate.

Also note that assignment and comparison can be considered built-in operations for equality, and that dereference and testing for NULL (the latter introduced in Section 4.2) can be considered *built-in functions* for references.

```
function plus-first                          function plus-next
    x₃ := x₁ + x₂                                return false
    return true


function less-first                          function less-next
    if x₁ < x₂ return true                       return false
    return false
```

Figure 4.2: Pseudocode for the "$\texttt{plus}(x_1, x_2.x_3)$" and "$\texttt{less}(x_1, x_2)$" access paths.

4.3.1 HASHING

The ability to represent *(computed) functions* as access paths can also be utilized to accommodate various data structures based on *hashing*:

Example 4.9 (Hash indices with separate chaining)   We illustrate this by showing how one can capture a hash index on $\texttt{dept}$ records, called $\texttt{deptidx-name}$, in which hashing is applied to department names, and in which hash conflicts are resolved by separate chaining. Physical design is captured as follows:

Access paths: $\{\texttt{hash}/2/1, \texttt{hasharraylookup}/2/1, \texttt{listscan}/2/1\} \subseteq S_A$.

Physical Constraints:

1. *For every $\texttt{dept}$ record in $\texttt{deptfile}$, hashing the contents the $\texttt{name}$ field yields a hash value, which can then be used to locate a linked list in the Hash Array by using $\texttt{hasharraylookup}$, which can then by traversed with $\texttt{listscan}$ to locate a reference to the $\texttt{dept}$ record:*

   $$\forall x, y.((\texttt{deptfile}(x) \wedge \texttt{dept-name}(x, y))$$
   $$\rightarrow \exists z, w.(\texttt{hash}(y, z) \wedge \texttt{hasharraylookup}(z, w) \wedge \texttt{listscan}(w, x))).$$

2. *The hash array covers the range of the hash function:*

   $$\forall x, y.(\texttt{hash}(x, y) \rightarrow \exists z.\texttt{hasharraylookup}(y, z)).$$

3. *The lists for separate chaining contain (references to) $\texttt{dept}$ records:*

   $$\forall x, y.(\texttt{listscan}(x, y) \rightarrow \texttt{deptfile}(y)).$$

Now, given a string value, we can use the above to efficient locate departments when supplied with a value for their name.   □

In general, a $\texttt{hash}$ function can result in conflicts, that is, can map different department names to a single value. The accompanying linked list implementation of chaining *reverses* this process. Note

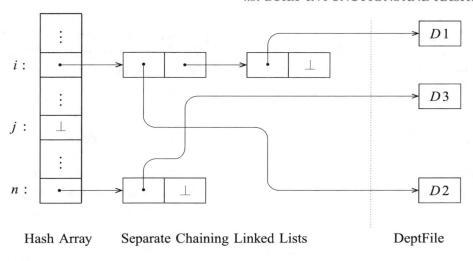

Figure 4.3: Hashing with separate chaining.

that the `listscan` access path represents *all* the lists used for the chaining of departments whose names have the same hash value: this is modelled as a two-place predicate that is interpreted as set of pairs of "references to the beginning of the list" (which is a parameter to the access path) paired with the contents of the cells of the list (that is returned by the access path), one pair per list cell. Hence, an empty list will not have any entry in the interpretation of this predicate.

Example 4.10   Consider a user query to *list department numbers and the names of their managers for departments that have a given name*:

$$\exists y, z.(\texttt{department}(x_1, p, y) \wedge \texttt{employee}(y, x_2, z))\{p\}.$$

A query plan implementing this query that uses the above hash index is given as follows:

$$\texttt{hash}(p, y) \wedge \texttt{hasharraylookup}(y, w) \wedge \texttt{listscan}(w, v)$$
$$\wedge \texttt{dept-num}(v, x_1) \wedge \texttt{dept-manager}(v, u) \wedge \texttt{emp-name}(u, x_2) .$$

The second line of the plan involves navigating through references in a fashion analogous to Example 4.2. □

The same `hash` function can be used in several hash tables. Doing so makes it possible to express query plans that behave as *hash joins* over such tables (see Exercise 4.3).

```
function pgscan-first                    function pgscan-next
   open(file)                               n := read(file, x₁, PGSIZE)
   return pgscan-next                       if n > 0 return true
                                            close(file)
                                            return false


function recscan-first                   function recscan-next
   i := 0                                   i := i + 1
   return recscan-next                      if (i > x₁.num) return false
                                            x₂ := address-of(x₁.buf[i])
                                            return true
```

Figure 4.4: Pseudocode for "pgscan(x_1)" and "recscan(x_1, x_2)" of "file".

4.4   TWO-LEVEL STORE

A hallmark of database management systems is their capacity for storing data in *external storage*, in particular on magnetic discs which must then be accessed in terms of *pages* at much higher cost than the main memory of an computer. We show that our methodology for physical design is sufficiently general to allow modeling such two-level store *without* having to build any such assumption into the technology from the start. The main idea is to *decompose* access paths that *scan* for records corresponding to entities into two access paths (per collection of records) as follows:

1. a first access path, pgscan/1/0, retrieves a sequence of pages of records; and

2. a second access path, recscan/2/1, takes such pages as argument and retrieves individual references to records from the given page.

The pseudocode for the access paths is presented in Figure 4.4. Note that we assume the layout for each page is to store the number of records held by the page followed by an array containing this number of records. (Alternative *page layouts* can be easily accommodated by straightforward modifications to the recscan access path code.)

The two access paths, coupled with appropriate integrity constraints and cost model ("accessing pgscan is expensive, accessing recscan is cheap"), then yield the expected behaviour of plans that access external storage.

Example 4.11   (A two-level employee file)   We illustrate this by replacing the access path empfile in our physical design of PAYROLL with a two-level file of employees:

Physical Signature: {emp-pgscan/1/0, emp-recscan/2/1} ⊆ S$_A$
    (empfile/1/0 is no longer an access path).

Constraints:

1. *Every reference to an* emp *record can be obtained by scanning some page of the two-level employee store*:

$$\forall x.(\texttt{empfile}(x) \equiv \exists y.\texttt{emp-recscan}(y, x)).$$

2. *Every record belongs to some page of the two level store*:

$$\forall x, y.(\texttt{emp-recscan}(y, x) \rightarrow \texttt{emp-pgscan}(y)).$$

3. *Every record belongs to a single page in two level store*:

$$\forall x, y_1, y_2.((\texttt{emp-recscan}(y_1, x) \wedge \texttt{emp-recscan}(y_2, x)) \rightarrow (y_1 \approx y_2)).$$

$\Box$

We now show how to obtain the behavior of a *nested loops join* in this setting by revisiting Example 4.4:

Example 4.12   Consider an earlier user query to *list pairs of employee numbers of employees with the same name*:

$$\exists y, z, w.(\texttt{employee}(x_1, y, z) \wedge \texttt{employee}(x_2, y, w)).$$

With this physical design, a query plan that implements this query in a way that accounts for two-level store is given as follows:

$$
\begin{aligned}
\exists y, z, w, v, p, q.\,(&\texttt{emppgscan}(p) \wedge \texttt{emppgscan}(q) \\
&\wedge \texttt{emprecscan}(p, y) \wedge \texttt{emp-num}(y, x_1) \wedge \texttt{emp-name}(y, w) \\
&\wedge \texttt{emprecscan}(q, z) \wedge \texttt{emp-num}(z, x_2) \wedge \texttt{emp-name}(z, v) \wedge \texttt{compare}(w, v)).
\end{aligned}
$$

Observe that the inner scan of emp records in this plan is performed once per *page* of the outer scan of emp record pages, and not per employee *record*. Indeed, without any additional query operators, the plan implements what is commonly referred to as *block nested loops join* in the database literature. $\Box$

4.4.1   TWO-LEVEL REFERENCES

The above solution to two-level storage is not quite satisfactory since it manifests an over-simplistic notion of a reference to a record in external storage. More realistically, such a reference is a pair of values consisting of a "reference to a page" coupled with an "offset of a record within a page". This can be captured by a refinement of the *two-level scan* by adding access paths that jointly allow retrieving a record given an external reference:

1. `pgload/2/1` that returns a page, given a page reference, and

2. `recload/3/2` that returns a reference to a record, given a page reference and a record offset.

Example 4.13 (two-level manager references)   Assume for this example that the `manager` reference field in `dept` records has been replaced with `mgrpg` and `mgroff` fields that encode a page reference and record offset to the external two level file of employees. The user query to *list the number and manager name for all departments,*

$$\exists y, z, w.(\texttt{department}(x_1, y, z) \wedge \texttt{employee}(z, x_3, w)),$$

can be now implemented by the plan:

$$\exists y, z, w, u, v.\,(\texttt{deptfile}(y) \wedge \texttt{dept-num}(y, x_1)$$
$$\wedge \texttt{dept-mgrpg}(y, z) \wedge \texttt{dept-mgroff}(y, w)$$
$$\wedge \texttt{emp-pgload}(z, u) \wedge \texttt{emp-recload}(u, w, v) \wedge \texttt{emp-num}(v, x_3)).$$

This assumes a matching modification of the physical constraints. In particular, constraint (10) in Example 4.1 should be replaced with the following constraint:

$$\forall x, y, z.(\texttt{department}(x, y, z) \rightarrow \exists w.\texttt{deptfile}(w) \wedge \texttt{dept-num}(w, x)$$
$$\wedge \texttt{dept-name}(w, y) \wedge \exists v, u.(\texttt{dept-mgrpg}(w, v) \wedge \texttt{dept-mgroff}(w, u)$$
$$\wedge \texttt{emp-pgload}(v, t) \wedge \texttt{emp-recload}(t, u, v) \wedge \texttt{emp-num}(v, z))).$$

In addition, predicates `emp-pgload` and `emp-rcload` must also be constrained to properly represent all *emp* records in ways that are analogous to how this is done for `emppgscan` and `emprcscan` in Example 4.11). □

4.4.2   ISAM INDEXING

We now show how to combine these ideas to model a B+-tree index with a fixed depth. Such indices are called ISAM indices in the literature, an acronym for *indexed sequential access method*. In particular, consider a physical design for PAYROLL in which all `dept` records are organized in an ISAM index on external store with the search key given by the name of a department. Assume that the number of such records is such that the index will consist of (at most) three levels of pages: a single root page, a set of index pages and a set of data pages. Records in the root page and index pages conform to the following `root` and `index` declarations:

```
record root of                    record index of
        string     namelow                string     namelow
        string     namehigh               string     namehigh
        reference  indexpg                reference  deptpg .
```

Records in the data pages conform to our initial design for `dept` records at the start of the chapter, but with the `manager` field replaced by the two fields `mgrpg` and `mgrrc` to encode page and offset references to department managers, as prescribed above:

```
record dept of
        integer    num
        string     name
        reference  mgrpg
        integer    mgroff .
```

Finally, assume that the logical design of PAYROLL has been revised slightly to include an additional constraint that no two distinct departments have the same name:

$$\forall x_1, x_2, y_1, y_2.(\exists z.(\texttt{department}(x_1, z, x_2) \land \texttt{department}(y_1, z, y_2))$$
$$\rightarrow ((x_1 \approx y_1) \land (x_2 \approx y_2))).$$

Appropriate access paths and constraints that capture the ability to find references to dept records that encode department entities implied by these records are then straightforward.

Example 4.14 (An ISAM index on department names)   Access paths and constraints that support a lookup capability to find page references and offsets within pages of dept records having a value of their name fields given by a parameter are defined as follows.

Physical Signature: Add the following to S_A together with the "field access" access paths induced by the above records (e.g., root-namehigh/2/1).

1. *It is possible to load the root page in a main memory buffer, if necessary, and return a reference to this page*:

   root-pgload/1/0 .

2. *Given a reference to the root page, it is possible to return the offsets of each* root *record in the page*:

   root-offscan/2/1 .

3. *Given a reference to the root page and an offset of a* root *record, it is possible to return a reference to the record*:

   root-recload/3/2 .

4. *Given a page reference to an index page, it is possible to load this page in a main memory buffer, if necessary, and return a reference to this page*:

   index-pgload/2/1 .

5. *Given a reference to an index page, it is possible to return the offsets of each* index *record in this page*:

   index-offscan/2/1 .

6. *Given a reference to an index page and an offset of an* index *record, it is possible to return a reference to the record*:

    index-recload/3/2 .

7. *Given a page reference to a department page, it is possible to load this page in a main memory buffer, if necessary, and return a reference to this page*:

    dept-pgload/2/1 .

8. *Given a reference to a department page, it is possible to return the offsets of each* dept *record in this page*:

    dept-offscan/2/1 .

9. *Given a reference to a department page and an offset of a* dept *record, it is possible to return a reference to the record*:

    dept-recload/3/2 .

Physical Constraints Σ' (a selection):

1. *Every* dept *record occurs in some department page*:

    $\forall x.(\exists y, z.\text{dept-recload}(x, y, z) \equiv \exists w.\text{dept-pgload}(w, x)).$

2. *There is an* index *record for each department page*:

    $\forall x.(\exists y.\text{dept-pgload}(x, y) \equiv \exists z, w.\text{index-recload}(z, w, x)).$

3. *Every* index *record occurs in some index page*:

    $\forall x.(\exists y, z.\text{index-recload}(x, y, z) \equiv \exists w.\text{index-pgload}(w, x)).$

4. *There is an* root *record for each index page*:

    $\forall x.(\exists y.\text{index-pgload}(x, y) \equiv \exists z, w.\text{root-recload}(z, w, x)).$

5. *Every* root *record occurs in some root page*:

    $\forall x.(\exists y, z.\text{root-recload}(x, y, z) \equiv \exists w.\text{root-pgload}(w, x)).$

6. *There is at most one root page*:

    $\forall x, y.((\text{root-pgload}(x) \wedge \text{root-pgload}(y)) \rightarrow (x \approx y)).$

7. *There is at least one root page*:

    $\exists x.\text{root-pgload}(x).$

8. *All department names in a given department page occur in the name range given by the* index *record for that page*:

$$\forall x, y, z, u, v, w, r, l, h, n.((\texttt{index-recload}(x, y, z)$$
$$\wedge\ \texttt{index-namelow}(z, l) \wedge \texttt{index-namehigh}(z, h)$$
$$\wedge\ \texttt{index-deptpg}(z, u) \wedge \texttt{dept-pgload}(u, v)$$
$$\wedge\ \texttt{dept-recload}(v, w, r) \wedge \texttt{dept-name}(r, n))$$
$$\rightarrow ((l \leq n) \wedge (n \leq h))).$$

9. *All name ranges in a given index page occur in the name range given by the* root *record for that page*:

$$\forall x, y, z, u, v, w, r, l_1, h_1, l_2, h_2.((\texttt{root-recload}(x, y, z)$$
$$\wedge\ \texttt{root-namelow}(z, l_1) \wedge \texttt{root-namehigh}(z, h_1)$$
$$\wedge\ \texttt{root-indexpg}(z, u) \wedge \texttt{index-pgload}(u, v)$$
$$\wedge\ \texttt{index-recload}(v, w, r) \wedge \texttt{index-namelow}(r, l_2))$$
$$\wedge\ \texttt{index-namehigh}(r, h_2))$$
$$\rightarrow ((l_1 \leq l_2) \wedge (h_2 \leq h_1))).$$

10. *A name range low value never exceeds a name range high value in any index record*:

$$\forall x, y, z, l, h.((\texttt{index-recload}(x, y, z)$$
$$\wedge\ \texttt{index-namelow}(z, l) \wedge \texttt{index-namehigh}(z, h))$$
$$\rightarrow (l \leq h)).$$

11. *No two name ranges in a given index page overlap*:

$$\forall x, y, z, w, l_1, h_1, l_2, h_2.((\texttt{index-recload}(x, y, z) \wedge \texttt{index-recload}(x, y, w)$$
$$\wedge\ \texttt{index-namelow}(z, l_1) \wedge \texttt{index-namehigh}(z, h_1)$$
$$\wedge\ \texttt{index-namelow}(w, l_2) \wedge \texttt{index-namehigh}(w, h_2)$$
$$\wedge\ (l_2 \leq h_1) \wedge (l_1 \leq h_2))$$
$$\rightarrow (z \approx w)).$$

Mapping Constraints Σ'':

1. *There is a page reference and offset of a* dept *record for every department*:

$$\forall x.(\exists y, z.\texttt{department}(x, y, z)$$
$$\equiv \exists u, v, w.(\texttt{dept-recload}(u, v, w) \wedge \texttt{dept-name}(w, x))).$$

Note that the last physical constraint above would not be justified were we to not have added a logical constraint prohibiting a common name for two or more departments.

Now consider a user query to *list of name of the manager of the department with a name given by a parameter x_1*:

$$\exists y, z, w.(\texttt{department}(y, x_1, z) \wedge \texttt{employee}(z, x_2, w)) \{x_1\}.$$

The query is implemented by the plan:

$$\exists p_1, o_1, p_2, o_2, p_3, o_3, p_4, o_4, r_1, r_2, r_3, r_4, r_5, r_6, r_7, l_1, h_1, l_2, h_2, n.($$
$$\texttt{root-pgload}(p_1) \wedge [\texttt{root-offscan}(p_1, o_1)]_1 \wedge \texttt{root-recload}(p_1, o_1, r_1)$$
$$\wedge \ \texttt{root-namelow}(r_1, l_1) \wedge \texttt{less}(l_1, x_1) \wedge \texttt{root-namehigh}(r_1, h_1) \wedge \texttt{lesseq}(x_1, h_1) \wedge \ !_1$$
$$\wedge \ \texttt{root-indexpg}(r_1, r_2)$$
$$\wedge \ \texttt{index-pgload}(r_2, p_2) \wedge [\texttt{index-offscan}(p_2, o_2)]_2 \wedge \texttt{index-recload}(p_2, o_2, r_3)$$
$$\wedge \ \texttt{index-namelow}(r_3, l_2) \wedge \texttt{less}(l_1, x_1) \wedge \texttt{index-namehigh}(r_3, h_2) \wedge \texttt{lesseq}(x_1, h_2) \wedge \ !_2$$
$$\wedge \ \texttt{index-deptpg}(r_3, r_4)$$
$$\wedge \ \texttt{dept-pgload}(r_4, p_3) \wedge [\texttt{dept-offscan}(p_3, o_3)]_3 \wedge \texttt{dept-recload}(p_3, o_3, r_5)$$
$$\wedge \ \texttt{dept-name}(r_5, n) \wedge \texttt{compare}(n, x_1) \wedge \ !_3$$
$$\wedge \ \texttt{dept-mgrpg}(r_5, r_6) \wedge \texttt{dept-mgroff}(r_6, o_4)$$
$$\wedge \ \texttt{emp-pgload}(r_6, o_4, p_4) \wedge \texttt{emp-recload}(p_4, o_4, r_7)$$
$$\wedge \ \texttt{emp-name}(r_7, x_2)$$
$$) .$$

Note that the cut operators are possible because of our revision to the logical design of PAYROLL requiring departments to have unique names. Additional cut operators could also have been added to reflect the functionality of loading a page, of computing a reference to a record in a page, of field access and of order comparison. For example, the subplan "$\texttt{root-namelow}(r_1, l_1)$" can be replaced by the subplan

$$([\texttt{root-namelow}(r_1, l_1)]_4 \wedge \ !_4).$$

$\square$

In this scenario, we have assumed that the ISAM index will require (at most) three levels of pages. It is straightforward to generalize the physical design to accommodate any number of levels for the index up to a constant maximum. In particular, one can start by replacing the index record declaration with a finite sequence of such declarations, $(\texttt{index}_1, \dots, \texttt{index}_n)$, in which the original deptpg field of an index record occurring in a page now containing $\texttt{index}_i$ records will now encode a reference to a page containing $\texttt{index}_{i+1}$ records when $i < n$. However, note it is not possible in FOL to further generalize this design to allow for an *arbitrary* number of levels.

4.5   SUMMARY

We have seen how a variety of more sophisticated ways to encode data commonly used in databases can be incorporated in a physical design without the need to introduce new query operators beyond what were introduced in the previous chapter. Pointers to records stored in disk pages, adding user defined functions to incorporate a new concrete domain, hash-based indexing and search trees in two-level store can all be introduced by adding new predicate symbols, access paths and constraints to an existing physical design.

4.6   BIBLIOGRAPHIC NOTES

Early work by Batory and Gotlieb [1982] looked into developing a unifying model of file access by databases, a topic that had already become diverse by that time. The topic was revisited in the 1990s by Hellerstein et al. [1995] and Tsatalos et al. [1996] who considered general abstractions of physical design for which such things as B+-trees were concrete instances.

4.7   EXERCISES WITH TOPICS FOR DISCUSSION

Exercise 4.1   Show an alternative physical design to that proposed in Example 4.5 that will allow employees that are not associated via predicate `works` with a department, and that is based on a *horizontal partition* of `emp` records. Define the appropriate access paths and integrity constraints. Also show how plans would look for the user queries in Example 4.6.

Exercise 4.2   Define physical design that handles constants as unary predicates. What access paths, if any, and constraints are needed?

Exercise 4.3   Departments with the same name via scanning the `hasharray`; design access paths and constraints and show a plan.

Exercise 4.4   Develop a physical design for three-level store. Discuss clustering.

Exercise 4.5   Develop a (part of) physical design, i.e., access path(s) and constraints, that simulate *buffered nested loops join*, nested loops join that reads left completely in a buffer and then scans right just once. Assume that the left (outer) argument is always an access path.

Exercise 4.6   Modify the physical design in Example 4.14 to allow both index and root records to encode departments.

CHAPTER 5

Query Compilation and Plan Synthesis

We have seen how FOL can be the basis for logical design, expressing user queries, augmenting a logical design with additional knowledge on how data is materially encoded, altogether called a physical design, and expressing low-level query plans over a physical design. Our primary objective in this chapter is to review algorithms that solve the problem of query compilation, that is, of automatically synthesizing query plans for user queries given the physical design for a database. Fundamentally, we study the following problem. Given

1. a user query Q over the signature S_L and

2. a physical design $\langle S_L \cup S_P, \Sigma \rangle$ over the signature $S_L \cup S_P$ defined by a set of constraints Σ and set of access paths $S_A \subseteq S_P$,

find a query plan $Q' \in \text{PLAN(S)}$ such that Q' implements the user query Q in theory Σ, that is, such that

$$\Sigma \models Q \lhd Q' .$$

In our setting, however, it might be possible that no such query plan exists, e.g., in the extreme case in which there are no access paths. In such cases, the appropriate course of action would be to at least inform the user that no plan can be found and that additional physical design is called for. Thus, part of the issue, and the issue we first address, is the question of whether or not any query plan exists for a user query.

5.1 BETH DEFINABILITY

A necessary condition for the existence of a query plan is closely tied to the question of whether or not the data represented by the available access paths is *sufficient* to answer the user query, that is, whether the answer to the query is *determined* solely by the interpretation of the available access paths. Formally, the condition can be expressed as follows:

Definition 5.1 (Beth Definability) Let $\langle S_L \cup S_P, \Sigma \rangle$ be a physical design with access paths S_A and Q a user query over S_L. We say that Q *is (Beth) definable in* $\langle S_L \cup S_P, \Sigma \rangle$ if $Q(\mathcal{I}_1) = Q(\mathcal{I}_2)$ for all interpretations $\mathcal{I}_1$ and $\mathcal{I}_2$ that satisfy Σ and such that $(R)^{\mathcal{I}_1} = (R)^{\mathcal{I}_2}$ for all non-logical parameters $R/m/n \in S_A$. $\square$

Moreover, definability of user queries with respect to a physical design can be tested syntactically as follows:

Theorem 5.2   Let Q be a user query, S_A a set of access paths, and Σ a set of constraints. Then Q is definable if and only if

$$\Sigma \cup \Sigma^* \models Q \to Q^* \, ,$$

where Σ^* and Q^* are copies of Σ and Q, respectively, in which all non-logical parameters *not present* in S_A are uniformly renamed (e.g., each such $R \in S - S_A$ is replaced by R^*, etc.).   □

In this way, definability can serve as a test to determine if the data *stored* in instances of access paths in a given physical design is sufficient, in principle, to answer the user query. Failing this condition indicates that the physical design, in particular the constraints and access paths, do not manifest sufficient material capability to answer the user query in question.

Example 5.3   We illustrate the technique by applying it to Example 3.2 from Chapter 3 where the integrity constraints are

$$\Sigma = \{ \ \forall x, y, z.(\texttt{employee}(x, y, z) \to \texttt{emp-array0}(z, x, y)),$$
$$\forall x, y, z.(\texttt{emp-array0}(z, x, y) \to \texttt{employee}(x, y, z)) \ \},$$

and $S_A = \{\texttt{emp-array0}/3/0\}$. Hence,

$$\Sigma \cup \Sigma^* = \{ \ \forall x, y, z.(\texttt{employee}(x, y, z) \to \texttt{emp-array0}(z, x, y)),$$
$$\forall x, y, z.(\texttt{emp-array0}(z, x, y) \to \texttt{employee}(x, y, z)),$$
$$\forall x, y, z.(\texttt{employee}^*(x, y, z) \to \texttt{emp-array0}(z, x, y)),$$
$$\forall x, y, z.(\texttt{emp-array0}(z, x, y) \to \texttt{employee}^*(x, y, z)) \ \},$$

and it is easy to see that, for the user query $\texttt{employee}(x, y, z)$, we have

$$\Sigma \cup \Sigma^* \models \forall x, y, z.\texttt{employee}(x, y, z) \to \texttt{employee}^*(x, y, z)$$

as required by the theorem. The result can be established using standard proof rules (such as modus ponens) applied on the following two assumptions in $\Sigma \cup \Sigma^*$:

1. $\forall x, y, z.(\texttt{employee}(x, y, z) \to \texttt{emp-array0}(z, x, y))$ and

2. $\forall x, y, z.(\texttt{emp-array0}(z, x, y) \to \texttt{employee}^*(x, y, z))$.

Hence, intuitively, $\texttt{emp-array0}$ is a candidate for a plan implementing the user query, and, since it satisfies the conditions induced by *binding patterns*, it is indeed a plan as expected.   □

In Section 5.3 we generalize this idea to *extracting* plan candidates from proofs to arbitrary Σ and Q. Note, however, that had the access path $\texttt{emp-array0}/3/0$ been missing, e.g., when $S_A = \{ \}$, the above logical implication would fail to hold and the query would not be definable.

Conversely, Beth definability in the above sense does not take into account the *particular restrictions* on access paths in terms of mandatory input parameters. Hence, a plan may still not exist.

Example 5.4   It is easy to see that the same reasoning leads to the conclusion that the query plan

$$\mathtt{emp\text{-}array2}(z, x, y)$$

is another candidate plan for user query $\mathtt{employee}(x, y, z)$. However, since the input variables of the plan do not correspond to the user query parameters (cf. Definition 3.8), the plan fails to qualify as an implementation of the user query. The opposite would hold if the user query were instead given as

$$\mathtt{employee}(x, y, z)\{x, z\} \;.$$

(In this case, the user query parameters match the plan input variables.)

□

We now consider a pair of algorithmic techniques in the following two sections that can be used to synthesize query plans.

5.2   CONJUNCTIVE QUERIES AND DEPENDENCIES

The first technique is centered around *conjunctive queries* (or SQL $\mathtt{select}$-blocks) and constraints that are formulated as *tuple generating dependencies* (TGDs).

5.2.1   THE CHASE

The basis of this technique is a classical approach for reasoning with conjunctive queries and dependencies called the *chase*. The main idea of the chase is given by the following theorem.

Theorem 5.5   (Chase Step)   Let Σ denote a given theory in FOL, and assume we are given the following:

1. a conjunctive query free of equality atoms: $\exists x_1. \cdots .\exists x_m.\varphi$,

2. a tuple generating dependency in Σ:

$$\forall x_1. \cdots .\forall x_i.(\exists x_{i+1}. \cdots .\exists x_j.\phi \rightarrow \exists x_{j+1}. \cdots .\exists x_k.\psi)$$

   and

3. a substitution θ such that $\phi_i\theta$ is an atom in φ for each atom ϕ_i in ϕ.

Then the following holds:

$$\Sigma \models (\exists x_1. \cdots .\exists x_m.\varphi) \equiv (\exists x_1. \cdots .\exists x_m.\varphi \wedge (\exists x_{j+1}. \cdots .\exists x_k.\psi)\theta).$$

$\square$

The formula that is the result of the chase step,

$$(\exists x_1. \cdots .\exists x_m.\varphi \wedge (\exists x_{j+1}. \cdots .\exists x_k.\psi)\theta) ,$$

is easily converted to a conjunctive query using a standard equivalence for FO formulae allowing existential quantification to commute with conjunction after renaming the bound variable if necessary. This observation often leads to syntactically equating conjunctive queries with sets of their atoms, and then distinguishing in some manner free variables and existentially quantified variables.

A repeated application of the *chase step* over all dependencies in Σ is called the *chase of Q with* Σ. is easy to see that the application of chase steps is confluent (up to renaming of variables) and thus any fair sequence of applying the individual chase steps for dependencies in Σ leads to the same (in the limit possibly infinite) expansion of the original conjunctive query.

5.2.2   NESTED LOOPS AND RIGHT-DEEP JOIN PLANS

The second facet of the chase-based synthesis algorithm is the following observation about the behaviour of nested loops joins.

Example 5.6   Consider three access paths $a/1/0, b/1/0$, and $c/1/0$, an interpretation $\mathcal{I}$ such that $(a)^{\mathcal{I}} = \{a_1, a_2\}, (b)^{\mathcal{I}} = \{b_1, b_2\}$, and $(c)^{\mathcal{I}} = \{c_1, c_2\}$, and two query plans,

$$a(x_1) \wedge (b(x_2) \wedge c(x_3))$$

and

$$(a(x_1) \wedge b(x_2)) \wedge c(x_3) .$$

Now consider the execution of these two plans in terms of *calls* to the `first` and `next` functions that implement the individual access paths. In particular, it is easy to see that the trace of function calls

```
a-first,  b-first,  c-first,  c-next,  c-next,
          b-next,   c-first,  c-next,  c-next,
          b-next,
a-next,   b-first,  c-first,  c-next,  c-next,
          b-next,   c-first,  c-next,  c-next,
          b-next,
a-next
```

corresponds to *both* of the above plans. Note that the `next` function is called twice: the second call always returns `false` to indicate that there are no more values in the corresponding access path. $\square$

This observation generalizes to arbitrary (syntactic trees of) conjunctions and shows that they can be replaced by a simple ordered list of conjuncts *without changing the trace behaviour* of the plan (see Exercise 5.1). Hence, when synthesizing query plans, it is sufficient to consider right-deep join plans only. These can be naturally represented by *ordered* lists of atoms.

5.2.3   CHASE AND PLAN SYNTHESIS

We use the chase to synthesize plans for the original user query Q with respect to a physical design $\langle S_L \cup S_P, \Sigma \rangle$ and access paths S_A. Since the construction proceeds in two steps, we need a characterization of the intermediate result. In particular, we say that a conjunctive query

$$\exists x_{j+1}. \cdots .\exists x_m.(\psi_1 \wedge \ldots \wedge \psi_k)$$

satisfies binding patterns for access paths S_A if $\psi_i \in S_P$ and if each variable occurring in the parameter positions of ψ_i is among the parameters of Q or among the variables in the non-parameter positions of some ψ_j for $j < i$. (Note that the ordering of the conjuncts in the query is significant for this definition.)

Now consider a physical design $\langle S_L \cup S_P, \Sigma \rangle$ and a conjunctive user query

$$Q = \exists x_1. \cdots .\exists x_m.\varphi\{x_{i_1}, \ldots, x_{i_\ell}\}$$

with parameters $\mathsf{Param}(Q) = \{x_{i_1}, \ldots, x_{i_\ell}\}$. Let $\mathrm{chase}_\Sigma(Q)$ be a chase of Q with Σ and Q' a conjunctive query

$$Q' = \exists y_1. \cdots .\exists y_t.\psi$$

such that

1. $\mathsf{Fv}(Q) = \mathsf{Fv}(Q')$,

2. Q' satisfies binding patterns for access paths S_A,

3. every atom ψ_i in ψ appears in $\mathrm{chase}_\Sigma(Q)$, and

4. for every atom φ_i in φ an atom φ_i' appears in $\mathrm{chase}_\Sigma(Q')$, where φ_i' is the same as φ_i except for names of existentially quantified variables of Q.

The above conditions allow us to conclude that $\Sigma \models Q \equiv Q'$ and that Q' can be used to construct a valid plan for the given physical design.

There are various ways to identify the atoms ψ_i of Q' in $\mathrm{chase}_\Sigma(Q)$ that depend primarily on whether the chase itself terminates.

- For terminating chase, one can look for all subsets that satisfy access path binding patterns in an a priori fashion. Note that, once a sufficient set Q' of atoms are found, there is no reason to look at supersets of Q'.

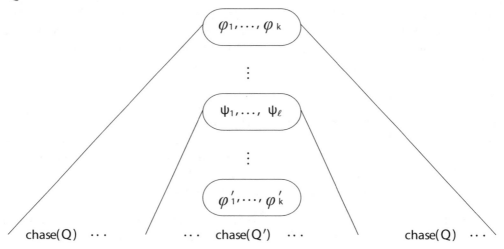

Figure 5.1: The chase.

- For non-terminating chase, one can interleave the chase of Q with search for the sets Q' of atoms for which there exists a total order that satisfies the syntactic conditions on plans imposed by binding patterns. However, note that selecting the first qualifying Q' might lead to suboptimal plans since further chasing of Q may possibly contain preferable access paths to data.

In practice, it is often necessary to run chase opportunistically to a predetermined limit before searching for the atoms to form the plan. Note that chase(Q') is contained in chase(Q). Hence, the chase of Q' can be found in $\text{chase}_\Sigma(Q)$ and thus the synthesis algorithm can proceed in only two main phases, steps 1 and 2 below.

1. Compute $\text{chase}_\Sigma(Q)$ to a given depth k.

2. Identify atoms of Q' *and* all consequences of these atoms in $\text{chase}_\Sigma(Q)$. This is equivalent to $\text{chase}_\Sigma(Q')$ to an appropriate depth depending on k.

3. Test if the set of atoms, considered as a conjunctive query, contains Q up to renaming of bound variables. If not, increase k and return to step 1.

4. Return Q'.

Figure 5.1 illustrates the overall process. Note that for non-terminating chase, extending the depth of search k does not require recomputing the chase from the start. One can simply extend the current chase in (1) by additional chase steps.

Example 5.7 (Chase and Field Navigation)   We show the process on the physical design introduced in Example 4.1. For the user query

$$Q = \exists y, z, u.(\texttt{employee}(x_1, x_2, y) \wedge \texttt{works}(x_1, z) \wedge \texttt{department}(z, x_3, u)),$$

one obtains as (part of) chase(Q) the following:

$\exists y, z, u, w, v.($
$\quad$ $\texttt{employee}(x_1, x_2, y) \wedge \texttt{works}(x_1, z) \wedge \texttt{department}(z, x_3, u) \wedge$
$\quad$ $\texttt{empfile}(w) \wedge \texttt{emp-num}(w, x_1) \wedge$ $\qquad\qquad\qquad$ using ($m1$)
$\quad$ $\texttt{emp-name}(w, x_2) \wedge$ $\qquad\qquad\qquad\qquad\qquad$ using ($m2$)
$\quad$ $\texttt{deptfile}(v) \wedge \texttt{dept-num}(v, z) \wedge$ $\qquad\qquad\qquad$ using ($m7$)
$\quad$ $\texttt{dept-name}(v, x_3) \wedge$ $\qquad\qquad\qquad\qquad\qquad$ using ($m8$)
$\quad$ $\texttt{emp-dept}(w, v) \wedge \ldots)$ $\qquad\qquad\qquad\qquad$ using ($m4$) .

We select

$$Q' = \exists w, v.(\texttt{empfile}(w) \wedge \texttt{emp-num}(w, x_1) \wedge \texttt{emp-name}(w, x_2)$$
$$\wedge \texttt{emp-dept}(w, v) \wedge \texttt{dept-name}(v, x_3)).$$

Now consider that (part of) chase(Q') is given by the following:

$\exists w, v, u_1, u_2, u_3, u_4.($
$\quad$ $\texttt{empfile}(w) \wedge \texttt{emp-num}(w, x_1) \wedge \texttt{emp-name}(w, x_2)$
$\qquad\qquad\qquad\qquad \wedge \texttt{emp-dept}(w, v) \wedge \texttt{dept-name}(v, x_3) \wedge$
$\quad$ $\texttt{emp-salary}(w, u_1) \wedge$ $\qquad\qquad\qquad\qquad\quad$ using ($p1c$)
$\quad$ $\texttt{employee}(x_1, x_2, u_1) \wedge$ $\qquad\qquad\qquad\qquad$ using ($m5$)
$\quad$ $\texttt{deptfile}(v) \wedge$ $\qquad\qquad\qquad\qquad\qquad\quad$ using ($p2$)
$\quad$ $\texttt{dept-num}(v, u_2) \wedge$ $\qquad\qquad\qquad\qquad\quad$ using ($p3a$)
$\quad$ $\texttt{works}(x_1, u_2) \wedge$ $\qquad\qquad\qquad\qquad\qquad$ using ($m6$)
$\quad$ $\texttt{dept-manager}(v, u_3) \wedge$ $\qquad\qquad\qquad\qquad$ using ($p3c$)
$\quad$ $\texttt{empfile}(u_3) \wedge$ $\qquad\qquad\qquad\qquad\qquad\quad$ using ($p4$)
$\quad$ $\texttt{emp-num}(u_3, u_4) \wedge$ $\qquad\qquad\qquad\qquad\quad$ using ($p1a$)
$\quad$ $\texttt{department}(u_2, x_3, u_4) \wedge \ldots)$ $\qquad\qquad\quad$ using ($m10$) .

Note that condition (4) is now satisfied since

$$Q\theta = (\texttt{employee}(x_1, x_2, u_1) \wedge \texttt{works}(x_1, u_2) \wedge \texttt{department}(u_2, x_3, u_4))$$

is now part of chase(Q'), where θ is given by the substitution

$$[x_1/x_1, x_2/x_2, x_3/x_3, u_1/y, u_2/z, u_4/u] .$$

□

5.2.4   EQUALITY-GENERATING DEPENDENCIES

Equality-generating dependencies, formulas of the form

$$\forall x_1. \cdots . \forall x_k. \phi \rightarrow x_i \approx x_j$$

can be used in the chase steps as well (as long as their preconditions are equality-free). However, they introduce equality atoms in the result of a chase step that need to be manipulated before the next chase step is applied as follows: for all equality atoms of the form $x_i \approx x_j$ in Q' (for $i < j$) we perform the following (equivalence-preserving) transformations:

1. both x_i and x_j are bound in Q': replace x_j by x_i in Q' and remove the equality atom from Q' and the existential quantifier for x_j;

2. x_i is bound and x_j is free in Q': replace x_i by x_j in Q' and remove the equality atom from Q' and the existential quantifier for x_i;

3. both x_i and x_j are free in Q': replace x_j by x_i in Q' except in the equality atom $x_i \approx x_j$ (and keep this atom in Q');

The above steps are repeated as long as Q' changes to account for transitivity of equality. The resulting formula is again a conjunctive query free of equalities, save those arising from (3) above that do not interfere with the chase procedure since variables x_j will only occur once in these atoms (see Exercise 5.2).

5.2.5   POST-PROCESSING: ASSIGNMENTS AND COMPARISONS

Note that a Q' computed by the *chase*, such as in Example 5.7, may not yet qualify as a query plan yet since it may not satisfy binding pattern conditions for nested loops.

Example 5.8   The user query from Example 4.4,

$$\exists y, z, w.(\texttt{employee}(x_1, y, z) \wedge \texttt{employee}(x_2, y, w)),$$

can be shown, using the chase, to be equivalent to

$$\exists y, v, w. (\texttt{empfile}(v) \wedge \texttt{emp-num}(v, x_1) \wedge \texttt{emp-name}(v, y)$$
$$\wedge \texttt{empfile}(w) \wedge \texttt{emp-num}(w, x_2) \wedge \texttt{emp-name}(w, y)).$$

To satisfy binding patterns, we post-process this plan candidate to the following plan by explicitly inserting a comparison operator:

$$\{\exists y, z, w, v. (\texttt{empfile}(v) \wedge \texttt{emp-num}(v, x_1) \wedge \texttt{emp-name}(v, y)$$
$$\wedge \texttt{empfile}(w) \wedge \texttt{emp-num}(w, x_2) \wedge \texttt{emp-name}(w, z) \wedge \texttt{compare}(y, z))\}.$$

This plan finally implements the user query from Example 4.4.   □

This procedure can be generalized to all cases in which we find Q' using the chase (see Exercise 5.3). Note that, in addition to the explicit insertion of comparisons, a top-level *duplicate elimination* operation will in general need to be added to Q' to ensure that the query plan implements the original user query (see Theorem 3.16 (4)). In the next subsection, we consider how to rewrite query plans to reduce and possibly avoid the overhead that this entails.

Assignments are only generated for equality atoms of the form $x_i \approx x_j$ resulting from the chase with EGDs (cf. Section 5.2.4). These atoms simply duplicate a binding of one variable to another one and are replaced by the $\texttt{assign}(x_j, x_i)$ atoms.

5.2.6   POST-PROCESSING: DUPLICATE ELIMINATION

Adding duplicate elimination unconditionally to any query plan is clearly unacceptable on performance grounds. In this subsection, we explore conditions in which this operator can be entirely eliminated or replaced with less expensive duplicate eliminating operations on subplans. For example, consider that employee numbers are *keys* for emp records in empfile, and that such values are therefore *unique* for distinct employee records in the physical design introduced in Chapter 4. Moreover, every emp record contains exactly one name field. When these observations are taken into account, simple intuition tells us that removing the *duplicate elimination* will not change the number of results produced by the plan from Example 5.8. Hence, it seems clear that the plan

$$\exists y, z, w, v.(\,\texttt{empfile}(v) \wedge \texttt{emp-num}(v, x_1) \wedge \texttt{emp-name}(v, y)$$
$$\wedge \texttt{empfile}(w) \wedge \texttt{emp-num}(w, x_2) \wedge \texttt{emp-name}(w, z) \wedge \texttt{compare}(y, z))$$

also implements the query from Example 4.4 with respect to the physical design in question. To make the above argument formal, we define the following rules for manipulating the *duplicate elimination* operator.

Theorem 5.9   (Duplicate Elimination Removal)   Let Σ be a physical design and Q_1 and Q_2 be two query plans. We write rules of the form $Q_1 \leftrightarrow Q_2$ as shorthand to indicate that

$$\Sigma \models Q \lhd Q_1 \text{ iff } \Sigma \models Q \lhd Q_2$$

holds for all user queries Q. Each of the following three rules holds:

$$\exists v_1, \ldots, v_n.(\gamma \wedge \{R(x_1, \ldots, x_k)\} \wedge \delta) \quad \leftrightarrow \quad \exists v_1, \ldots, v_n.(\gamma \wedge R(x_1, \ldots, x_k) \wedge \delta)$$

$$\exists v_1, \ldots, v_n.(\gamma \wedge \{\varphi \wedge \psi\} \wedge \delta) \quad \leftrightarrow \quad \exists v_1, \ldots, v_n.(\gamma \wedge \{\varphi\} \wedge \{\psi\} \wedge \delta)$$

$$\exists v_1, \ldots, v_n.(\gamma \wedge \{\exists x.\varphi\} \wedge \delta) \quad \underset{\mathcal{C}}{\leftrightarrow} \quad \exists v_1, \ldots, v_n.(\gamma \wedge \exists x.\{\varphi\} \wedge \delta)$$

where condition $\mathcal{C}$ on the third rule is satisfied if

$$(\Sigma \cup \{\mathsf{Uq}(\gamma \wedge \varphi[y_1/x] \wedge \varphi[y_2/x] \wedge \delta)\}) \models (y_1 \approx y_2),$$

and where $y_1, y_2 \notin \mathsf{Fv}(\gamma \wedge \varphi \wedge \delta)$, $n \geq 0$, and γ and δ are plans that stand, respectively, for the atoms preceding and following the subformula being modified (or the no-op plan $\top$ when there are no such atoms). $\square$

The intuition underlying the condition on the third rule is that duplicate elimination commutes with existential quantification when the quantified variable is *functionally dependent* on the output of the subquery and on any additional variables that appear in a surrounding context.

Example 5.10   Combining the rules in Theorem 5.9 with associativity of the nested loop join operator (see Theorem 3.16) and with an additional rule unrelated to duplicate elimination,

$$\exists z.(\varphi \wedge \psi) \underset{z \notin \mathsf{Fv}(\varphi)}{\leftrightarrow} (\varphi \wedge \exists z.\psi)$$

enables us to formally justify our introductory claims of this subsection by the following argument.

$\{\exists y, z, w, v.(\texttt{empfile}(v) \wedge \texttt{emp-num}(v, x_1) \wedge \texttt{emp-name}(v, y)$
$\quad \wedge\ \texttt{empfile}(w) \wedge \texttt{emp-num}(w, x_2) \wedge \texttt{emp-name}(w, z) \wedge \texttt{compare}(y, z))\}$

$\leftrightarrow \exists y.\{\exists z, w, v.(\texttt{empfile}(v) \wedge \texttt{emp-num}(v, x_1) \wedge \texttt{emp-name}(v, y)$
$\quad \wedge\ \texttt{empfile}(w) \wedge \texttt{emp-num}(w, x_2) \wedge \texttt{emp-name}(w, z) \wedge \texttt{compare}(y, z))\}$

$\leftrightarrow \cdots$

$\leftrightarrow \exists y, z, w, v.\{(\texttt{empfile}(v) \wedge \texttt{emp-num}(v, x_1) \wedge \texttt{emp-name}(v, y)$
$\quad \wedge\ \texttt{empfile}(w) \wedge \texttt{emp-num}(w, x_2) \wedge \texttt{emp-name}(w, z) \wedge \texttt{compare}(y, z))\}$

$\leftrightarrow \exists y, z, w, v.(\{\texttt{empfile}(v)\} \wedge \{(\texttt{emp-num}(v, x_1) \wedge \texttt{emp-name}(v, y)$
$\quad \wedge\ \texttt{empfile}(w) \wedge \texttt{emp-num}(w, x_2) \wedge \texttt{emp-name}(w, z) \wedge \texttt{compare}(y, z))\})$

$\leftrightarrow \exists y, z, w, v.(\texttt{empfile}(v) \wedge \{(\texttt{emp-num}(v, x_1) \wedge \texttt{emp-name}(v, y)$
$\quad \wedge\ \texttt{empfile}(w) \wedge \texttt{emp-num}(w, x_2) \wedge \texttt{emp-name}(w, z) \wedge \texttt{compare}(y, z))\})$

$\leftrightarrow \cdots$

$\leftrightarrow \exists y, z, w, v.(\texttt{empfile}(v) \wedge \texttt{emp-num}(v, x_1) \wedge \texttt{emp-name}(v, y)$
$\quad \wedge\ \texttt{empfile}(w) \wedge \texttt{emp-num}(w, x_2) \wedge \texttt{emp-name}(w, z) \wedge \texttt{compare})(y, z)\ .$

The first step is justified by observing that y is *functionally dependent* on x_1 since employee numbers identify employees and since employees have exactly one name. Similar arguments apply for the remaining cases. $\square$

5.2.7   POST-PROCESSING: CUT INSERTION

The rules we have so far, that relate to our duplicate elimination operator, are bidirectional. Thus, they also determine situations in which such operators may be *added* to a query plan. This is useful when formulating additional rules that determine when cut operators can be inserted in conjunctive query plans without any impact on their ability to implement user queries.

Theorem 5.11   (Cut Introduction and Named Cut)   Let Σ be a physical design. Then the following rule holds:

$$\exists v_1, \ldots, v_m.(\gamma \wedge \{\varphi\} \wedge \psi \wedge \delta) \quad \underset{\mathcal{C}}{\leftrightarrow} \quad \exists v_1, \ldots, v_m.(\gamma \wedge [\varphi]_i \wedge \psi \wedge !_i \wedge \delta)$$

where condition $\mathcal{C}$ is satisfied if

$$\Sigma \cup \{\mathsf{Uq}(\gamma \wedge (\varphi \wedge \psi)[y_1/x_1, \ldots, y_k/x_k] \wedge (\varphi \wedge \psi)[z_1/x_1, \ldots, z_k/x_k])\} \models (y_i \approx z_i)$$

for all $0 < i \leq k$, where $m \geq 0$, $\{x_1, \ldots, x_k\} = \mathsf{Out}(\varphi)$, and where $\{y_1, \ldots, y_k\}$ and $\{z_1, \ldots, z_k\}$ are sets of fresh variables.   □

The intuition underlying the condition on this rule is that the output variables of subplan ϕ are *functionally determined* by variables and conditions that occur prior to subplan δ.

Example 5.12   This new rule suffices to demonstrate how the query plan in Example 3.11 can be synthesized by the following argument:

$$\exists u, v.(\texttt{emp-array0}(u, y, v) \wedge \texttt{compare}(x, u) \wedge \texttt{compare}(z, v))$$

$$\leftrightarrow \exists u, v.(\{\texttt{emp-array0}(u, y, v)\} \wedge \texttt{compare}(x, u) \wedge \texttt{compare}(z, v))$$

$$\leftrightarrow \exists u, v.([\texttt{emp-array0}(u, y, v)]_1 \wedge \texttt{compare}(x, u) \wedge !_1 \wedge \texttt{compare}(z, v)).$$

□

5.2.8   EXTENSIONS TO CHASE: BEYOND CONJUNCTIVE QUERIES

It is straightforward to expand the family of dependencies beyond tuple generating dependencies with a straightforward generalization of the chase procedure. The additional varieties of dependencies that become possible with this generalization are as follows.

Coverage dependencies:

$$\forall x_1. \cdots .\forall x_k.(\exists x_{k+1}. \cdots .\exists x_n.\phi) \rightarrow$$
$$((\exists x_{k+1}. \cdots .\exists x_{n_1}.\psi_1) \vee \ldots \vee (\exists x_{k+1}. \cdots .\exists x_{n_m}.\psi_m)) .$$

Denial dependencies:

$$\forall x_1. \cdots .\forall x_k.(\exists x_{k+1}. \cdots .\exists x_n.\phi) \rightarrow \mathsf{false}$$

where false stands for an unsatisfiable formula, e.g., $p \wedge \neg p$.

The more general chase procedure accommodates such additional dependencies by now viewing the chase procedure as something that maps sets of conjunctive queries to sets of conjunctive queries. This assumes that the sets denote disjunctions of member conjunctive queries, and that the implicit disjunctions are eventually replaced with concatenation operations.

The new chase works by incorporating the following.

1. Disjunctions in the result of the chase step are distributed over conjunctions and existential quantifiers in order to obtain a disjunction of conjunctive queries.

2. All disjuncts in which the atom false appears are then deleted.

Note that these steps predispose the expanded query to further applications of chase on each of the disjuncts individually. The remainder of the procedure proceeds as in the original chase: each of the sub-chases must imply the user query. Again, the resulting plans are then combined with concatenation operators to obtain a query plan.

Example 5.13   Continuing with Example 4.7, the extended chase obtains the following plan:

$$\{\exists y.(\texttt{empfile-mid}(y) \land \texttt{emp-num}(y, x_1)) \lor \exists y.(\texttt{empfile-low}(y)) \land \texttt{emp-num}(y, x_1))\}.$$

Note that the common subexpression emp-num is no longer factored from the concatenation. Moreover, for the extended chase to be applicable, the constraints that partition the emp records must be formulated as dependencies (see Exercise 5.4).   □

Note that the new chase will only synthesize positive query plans that are concatenations of conjunctive query plans. Hence, the second part of Example 4.7 cannot be obtained using the extended chase. More significantly, this shortcoming cannot be fully remedied by (possibly further) extensions to the chase (we demonstrate this in Section 5.3). Also, the results of the extended chase must still undergo post-processing in a similar fashion to the conjunctive case. To reason about duplicates, however, it is now necessary to reason about pairwise disjointness of conjunctive queries under the physical design, a task that we leave for Section 5.3.3 where a more general setting is considered.

5.3   FIRST-ORDER QUERIES AND CONSTRAINTS

Our second technique for plan synthesis is based on a constructive approach to synthesizing *Craig interpolants*. This is an alternative strategy to one that considers adding extensions to the basic chase algorithm. As we shall see, it is also more powerful than any of the chase-based procedures that were considered in the previous section.

To see why a more powerful approach is needed, we present an example of a conjunctive user query coupled with a physical design that consists entirely of tuple generating dependencies and access paths that have no input variables.

Example 5.14   Let $\langle \mathsf{S_L} \cup \mathsf{S_P}, \Sigma \rangle$ be a physical design defined as follows:

- the logical signature: $\mathsf{S_L} = \{R/2\}$,

- the physical signature and access paths: $\mathsf{S_P} = \mathsf{S_A} = \{V_1/2/0, V_2/2/0, V_3/2/0\}$, and

- the constraints $\Sigma = \{ \ \forall x, y.(V_1(x, y) \equiv \exists u, w.(R(u, x) \wedge R(u, w) \wedge R(w, y))),$
  $\forall x, y.(V_2(x, y) \equiv \exists u, w.(R(x, u) \wedge R(u, w) \wedge R(w, y))),$
  $\forall x, y.(V_3(x, y) \equiv \exists u.(R(x, u) \wedge R(u, y)))$ $\}$.

Also let Q denote the conjunctive user query

$$\exists u, v, w.(R(u, x) \wedge R(u, w) \wedge R(w, v) \wedge R(v, y)) .$$

An equivalent user query to Q can be formulated in terms of the three predicates that are access paths, V_1, V_2 and V_3, as follows:

$$\exists u.(V_1(x, u) \wedge \forall w.(V_3(w, u) \rightarrow V_2(w, y))).$$

Another user query that is also equivalent to Q, again, only with non-logical parameters that are access paths, is given by:

$$\exists u, v.(V_1(x, u) \wedge V_3(v, u) \wedge V_2(v, y) \wedge \forall w.(V_3(w, u) \rightarrow V_2(w, y))).$$

Standard equivalences in FOL can then be applied to this to obtain a query plan that implements Q.

$$\exists u, v.\{(V_1(x, u) \wedge V_3(v, u) \wedge V_2(v, y) \wedge \neg \exists w.(V_3(w, u) \wedge \neg V_2(w, y)))\}.$$

In general, it is known that there does not exist a *positive* user query equivalent to Q, that is, a user query devoid of any reference to either negation or universal quantification. □

Again, note that the user query in this example is a conjunctive query, and that all constraints can be captured as tuple generating dependencies. Hence, it is particularly noteworthy that none of the chase procedures we have reviewed is able to find this plan (cf. Section 5.2.8).

5.3.1   INTERPOLATION

The basis of this new and more powerful technique is *interpolation* as characterized by the logician Craig.

Theorem 5.15   (Craig)   Let φ and ψ be WFFs. Then $\models \varphi \rightarrow \psi$ implies that there is a WFF η that contains only non-logical symbols common to both φ and ψ, called the *interpolant*, such that $\models \varphi \rightarrow \eta \rightarrow \psi$. □

Craig's theorem applies in a straightforward way to the criterion for query definability given by Theorem 5.2:

$$\Sigma \cup \Sigma^* \models Q \rightarrow Q^* \text{ implies } \models ((\wedge\Sigma) \wedge Q) \rightarrow ((\wedge\Sigma^*) \rightarrow Q^*) ,$$

where, e.g., $\wedge\Sigma$ is the conjunction constructed from all constraints in Σ. (Note that this assumes Σ is finite. One needs to appeal to compactness if this is not the case, if Σ is infinite.) Hence, using Theorem 5.15 we have

$$\models ((\wedge\Sigma) \wedge Q) \to Q' \to ((\wedge\Sigma^*) \to Q^*), \tag{5.1}$$

and in turn

$$\Sigma \cup \Sigma^* \models Q \to Q' \to Q^* \text{ (and by symmetry } \Sigma \cup \Sigma^* \models Q^* \to Q' \to Q).$$

Thus, one obtains an interpolant Q' equivalent to Q under the schema constraints and containing only predicates that are also access paths. However, not any interpolant will suffice. As was the case with chase-based procedures and as Example 5.14 illustrates, it remains necessary to ensure that a query plan can be easily derived from Q'. We elaborate on this in Section 5.3.3.

5.3.2   INTERPOLANTS CONSTRUCTIVELY

We now show one way to compute interpolants in the *sequent calculus*. In particular, to obtain Q' in 5.1 observe that, since

$$\models ((\wedge\Sigma) \wedge Q) \to ((\wedge\Sigma^*) \to Q^*),$$

we have

$$((\wedge\Sigma) \wedge Q) \models ((\wedge\Sigma^*) \to Q^*).$$

It therefore follows that the sequent

$$((\wedge\Sigma) \wedge Q) \vdash ((\wedge\Sigma^*) \to Q^*)$$

has a cut-free proof in the sequent calculus (see Figure 5.2 for the inference rules of the calculus). From such a proof of the above assertion, an interpolant Q' can be mechanically extracted. Indeed, the proof rules of the cut-free sequent calculus presented in Figure 5.2 are enriched for this task: our notation adorns standard sequents of the form "$\Gamma \vdash \Delta$" with interpolant extraction adornment of the form "$\rightsquigarrow \varphi$". Note that if a sequent proof of $\Gamma \vdash \Delta$ exists, then a cut-free proof also exists, and every such proof can be subsequently adorned with the interpolant extraction adornments.

Theorem 5.16   Let Γ and Δ be finite sets of WFFs, and assume the sequent $\Gamma \vdash \Delta \rightsquigarrow \varphi$ can be derived using the proof rules given in Figure 5.2. Then

$$\models (\wedge\Gamma) \to \varphi \to (\vee\Delta), \tag{5.2}$$

where $\wedge\Gamma$ (resp. $\vee\Delta$) denotes the conjunctions (resp. disjunctions) of all formulas in the set Γ (resp. Δ). $\qquad\square$

Axioms:

$$\Gamma, \varphi \vdash \varphi, \Delta \rightsquigarrow \varphi \qquad \Gamma \vdash \varphi, \neg\varphi, \Delta \rightsquigarrow \top \qquad \Gamma, \varphi, \neg\varphi \vdash \Delta \rightsquigarrow \bot$$

where $\top$ stands for a tautology (true) and $\bot$ for a contradiction (false).

Propositional Rules:

$$\frac{\Gamma \vdash \varphi_1, \Delta \rightsquigarrow \psi_1 \quad \Gamma \vdash \varphi_2, \Delta \rightsquigarrow \psi_2}{\Gamma \vdash \varphi_1 \wedge \varphi_2, \Delta \rightsquigarrow \psi_1 \wedge \psi_2} \qquad \frac{\Gamma, \varphi_1, \varphi_2 \vdash \Delta \rightsquigarrow \psi}{\Gamma, \varphi_1 \wedge \varphi_2 \vdash \Delta \rightsquigarrow \psi}$$

$$\frac{\Gamma, \varphi_1 \vdash \Delta \rightsquigarrow \psi_1 \quad \Gamma, \varphi_2 \vdash \Delta \rightsquigarrow \psi_2}{\Gamma, \varphi_1 \vee \varphi_2 \vdash \Delta \rightsquigarrow \psi_1 \vee \psi_2} \qquad \frac{\Gamma \vdash \varphi_1, \varphi_2, \Delta \rightsquigarrow \psi}{\Gamma \vdash \varphi_1 \vee \varphi_2, \Delta \rightsquigarrow \psi}$$

where WFFs of the form $\neg(\varphi_1 \wedge \varphi_2)$ and $\neg(\varphi_1 \vee \varphi_2)$ are treated as $(\neg\varphi_1) \vee (\neg\varphi_2)$ and $(\neg\varphi_1) \wedge (\neg\varphi_2)$, respectively.

First-order Quantifiers:

$$\frac{\Gamma, \varphi[t/x] \vdash \Delta \rightsquigarrow \psi}{\Gamma, \forall x.\varphi \vdash \Delta \rightsquigarrow \psi'} \qquad \frac{\Gamma \vdash \varphi[z/x], \Delta \rightsquigarrow \psi}{\Gamma \vdash \forall x.\varphi, \Delta \rightsquigarrow \psi}$$

$$\frac{\Gamma, \varphi[z/x] \vdash \Delta \rightsquigarrow \psi}{\Gamma, \exists x.\varphi \vdash \Delta \rightsquigarrow \psi} \qquad \frac{\Gamma \vdash \varphi[t/x], \Delta \rightsquigarrow \psi}{\Gamma \vdash \exists x.\varphi, \Delta \rightsquigarrow \psi''}$$

where t is a term, z a variable not in $\Gamma \cup \Delta \cup \{\varphi\}$ and where ψ' and ψ'' are $\forall x.\psi$ and $\exists x.\psi$, if t does not appear in Γ and Δ, respectively; and ψ otherwise. $\varphi[t/x]$ denotes the WFF resulting from syntactic substitution of the term t for the variable x in the WFF φ. WFFs of the form $\neg\exists x.\varphi$ and $\neg\forall x.\varphi$ are treated as $\forall x.\neg\varphi$ and $\exists x.\neg\varphi$, respectively.

Equality: We add congruences as additional constraints to Σ:

$$\forall x, y, z_1, \ldots, z_{k-1}.x \approx y \rightarrow$$
$$(R(z_1, \ldots, z_i, x, z_{i+1}, \ldots, z_{k-1}) \leftrightarrow R(z_1, \ldots, z_i, y, z_{i+1}, \ldots, z_{k-1}))$$

for each R/k predicate symbol in $\mathsf{S_L} \cup \mathsf{S_P} \cup \{\approx /2\}$ and $0 \leq i < k$. Note that this way the equalities will naturally participate in the construction of the interpolant.

Figure 5.2: Cut-free sequent proof rules and interpolant extraction.

Note that (5.2) is essentially what is needed to construct Q' according to (5.1) with the help of Theorem 5.15.

Example 5.17   Consider a physical design introduced in Example 3.2 from Chapter 3 for the PAYROLL system in which Σ is given by

$$\{ \forall x, y, z.(\texttt{employee}(x, y, z) \rightarrow \texttt{emp-array0}(z, x, y)),$$
$$\forall x, y, z.(\texttt{emp-array0}(z, x, y) \rightarrow \texttt{employee}(x, y, z)) \},$$

and S_A by $\{\texttt{emp-array0/3/0}\}$. A derivation of an interpolant using this calculus for the user query Q given by

$$\exists x.\texttt{employee}(x, x_1, x_2)$$

is shown in Figure 5.3. As required, only the access path $\texttt{emp-array0}$ occurs as a non-logical parameter in the interpolant, from which a query plan that implements Q is immediately obtained.

□

5.3.3   INTERPOLANTS VS. PLANS

Just as with chase procedures, interpolation will find a well-formed formula Q' that is equivalent to a given user query Q and that satisfies the syntactic condition that all non-logical parameters occurring in Q' are access paths. After rewriting sub-formulae of the form "$\forall x.\varphi$" in Q' with "$\neg\exists x.\neg\varphi$", it remains possible that Q' will not lead directly to a query plan that implements Q due to violations of binding pattern rules (see Chapter 3). One way to remedy this is by verifying the conditions imposed on the In and Out sets of variables after an interpolant is generated and, in the case of failure, searching for an alternative interpolant. Another way is to interleave checks that binding pattern rules are satisfied with the construction of the interpolant itself (see Exercise 5.5).

There are additional opportunities for post-processing of an interpolant, among them:

- factoring common subexpressions,

- removing *duplicate elimination* operators, and

- *cut insertion.*

Just as with binding pattern rules, it is possible to incorporate any of these opportunities into the interpolation process itself. We illustrate this in the case of common subexpressions.

Example 5.18   Consider a user query $a(x) \wedge a(x)$ in a setting where $a/1/0 \in S_A$ with no additional schema constraints available. It is easy to see that this query itself could serve as a plan. However, there is another plan that (also) implements this user query, namely, $a(x)$. Note that this alternative plan is commonly preferable (as it *scans* a only once). It is an easy exercise, however, to see that

$$
\dfrac{
\begin{array}{c}
\dfrac{
\begin{array}{c}
\mathsf{e}(s,x_1,x_2),\; \mathsf{e}^*(s,x_1,x_2),\\
\mathsf{a}(x_2,s,x_1) \vdash \exists x.\mathsf{e}^*(x,x_1,x_2),\; \neg\mathsf{e}^*(s,x_1,x_2) \rightsquigarrow \top
\end{array}
}{
\begin{array}{c}
\mathsf{e}(s,x_1,x_2),\\
\mathsf{a}(x_2,s,x_1) \vdash \exists x.\mathsf{e}^*(x,x_1,x_2),\\
\mathsf{a}(x_2,s,x_1)
\end{array}
\qquad
\begin{array}{c}
\mathsf{e}(s,x_1,x_2),\\
\mathsf{a}(x_2,s,x_1) \vdash \exists x.\mathsf{e}^*(x,x_1,x_2),\\
\neg\mathsf{e}^*(s,x_1,x_2)
\end{array}
}
\end{array}
}{
\begin{array}{c}
\mathsf{e}(s,x_1,x_2),\\
\mathsf{a}(x_2,s,x_1) \vdash \exists x.\mathsf{e}^*(x,x_1,x_2),\\
\mathsf{a}(x_2,s,x_1) \qquad \exists x,y,z.(\mathsf{a}(z,x,y)\wedge\neg\mathsf{e}^*(x,y,z)) \rightsquigarrow \mathsf{a}(x_2,s,x_1)
\end{array}
}
$$

$$
\dfrac{
\begin{array}{c}
\mathsf{e}(s,x_1,x_2),\\
\mathsf{a}(x_2,s,x_1) \vdash \exists x.\mathsf{e}^*(x,x_1,x_2),\\
\exists x,y,z.(\mathsf{a}(z,x,y)\wedge\neg\mathsf{e}^*(x,y,z)) \rightsquigarrow \mathsf{a}(x_2,s,x_1)
\end{array}
}{
\begin{array}{c}
\mathsf{e}(s,x_1,x_2),\\
\neg\mathsf{e}(s,x_1,x_2) \vdash \exists x.\mathsf{e}^*(x,x_1,x_2),\\
\exists x,y,z.(\mathsf{a}(z,x,y)\wedge\neg\mathsf{e}^*(x,y,z)) \rightsquigarrow \bot
\end{array}
}
$$

$$
\dfrac{
\begin{array}{c}
\mathsf{e}(s,x_1,x_2),\\
\neg\mathsf{e}(s,x_1,x_2)\vee\mathsf{a}(x_2,s,x_1) \vdash \exists x.\mathsf{e}^*(x,x_1,x_2),\\
\exists x,y,z.(\mathsf{a}(z,x,y)\wedge\neg\mathsf{e}^*(x,y,z)) \rightsquigarrow \mathsf{a}(x_2,s,x_1)
\end{array}
}{
\begin{array}{c}
\mathsf{e}(s,x_1,x_2),\\
\forall x,y,z.(\neg\mathsf{e}(x,y,z)\vee\mathsf{a}(z,x,y)) \vdash \exists x.\mathsf{e}^*(x,x_1,x_2),\\
\forall x,y,z.(\neg\mathsf{e}(x,y,z)\vee\mathsf{a}(z,x,y)) \;\; \exists x,y,z.(\mathsf{a}(z,x,y)\wedge\neg\mathsf{e}^*(x,y,z)) \rightsquigarrow \exists x.\mathsf{a}(x_2,x,x_1)
\end{array}
}
$$

Figure 5.3: Derivation of an interpolant.

applying the interpolation proof rules on the above user query cannot lead to the desired outcome: intuitively, there will be at least two a's in the interpolant.

However, we can *modify* the physical design as follows:

1. we replace the access paths with *new* symbol aa/1 that becomes an access paths in the new setting instead of a,

2. we add constraints that associate the new symbol with the original one, $\forall x.a(x) \equiv aa(x)$, and

3. we add certain *tautologies* to the schema constraints, for the purposes of this example $\forall x.\neg a(x) \lor a(x)$, and perhaps others.

Now we can, during the construction of an interpolant, use the tautology together with the inferences of the form $\Gamma \vdash \varphi, \neg\varphi, \Delta \rightsquigarrow \top$ and $\Gamma, \varphi, \neg\varphi \vdash \Delta \rightsquigarrow \bot$ to *eliminate* multiple occurrences of an symbol with no penalty incurred in the interpolant as the $\top$ and $\bot$ symbols can be easily eliminated from the resulting interpolant. We can, for example, construct an interpolant as follows (we omit the parameter "x", the associated quantifier rules, and constraints not involved in the proof to focus on the essentials of the idea):

$$
\cfrac{
\cfrac{
\cfrac{
\cfrac{a,a,\neg a, \atop \neg a \lor aa \vdash \cfrac{a^*\wedge a^*,}{aa \wedge \neg a^*} \rightsquigarrow \bot}{a \wedge a, \neg a \atop \neg a \lor aa \vdash \cfrac{a^*\wedge a^*,}{aa \wedge \neg a^*} \rightsquigarrow \bot}
\qquad
\cfrac{\cfrac{a\wedge a, \atop a, aa \vdash a^*,\neg a^* \rightsquigarrow \top}{a\wedge a, \atop a, aa \vdash \cfrac{a^*\wedge a^*,}{\neg a^*} \rightsquigarrow \top} \quad \cfrac{a\wedge a, \atop a, \neg a \vdash \cfrac{a^*\wedge a^*,}{aa\wedge\neg a^*} \rightsquigarrow \bot}{} }{a\wedge a, a, \atop \neg a \lor aa \vdash \cfrac{a^*\wedge a^*,}{aa\wedge\neg a^*} \rightsquigarrow aa}
}{}
\qquad
\cfrac{\cfrac{a\wedge a, \atop a, aa \vdash a^*,\neg a^* \rightsquigarrow \top}{a\wedge a, \atop a, aa \vdash \cfrac{a^*\wedge a^*,}{aa} \rightsquigarrow aa} \quad \cfrac{a\wedge a, \atop a, aa \vdash \cfrac{a^*\wedge a^*,}{aa\wedge\neg a^*} \rightsquigarrow aa}{}}{}
}{
a \wedge a, \atop \neg a \lor a, \neg a \lor aa \vdash \cfrac{a^*\wedge a^*,}{aa\wedge\neg a^*} \rightsquigarrow aa
}
$$

Note how the tautology $\forall x.a \lor \neg a$ was used to "trade" two a's in the user query (left and middle parts of the proof, in particular where the formula $a^* \wedge a^*$ is processed) for a single one in the rest of the proof derivation.   □

Note that the same approach can be used no matter how name $a(x)$ appear (positively) in the user query: they can be all factored using the same technique (see exercise 5.6). The example can be also generalized to accommodate distributivity by factoring $a(x)$ in

$$(a(x) \wedge b(x)) \lor (a(x) \wedge c(x))$$

(see Exercise 5.7) and to other structural transformations such as *join reordering* (see Exercise 5.8).

5.3.4   INTERPOLANTS AND DUPLICATES

We extend the technique for manipulating the *duplicate elimination* operator introduced in Section 5.2.6 to all plans. However, unlike the case of conjunctive queries, we can no longer rely on the existence of a normal form of plans. Therefore, we define the notion of *context* to abstract the *remainder* of the plan that surrounds the (sub-)plan that is being manipulated.

Definition 5.19   (Context)   Let Q be a plan that contains a subplan Q_1. We then write $Q[Q_1]$ and call $Q[]$ (Q in which Q_1 has been replaced by a placeholder []) a *context*.

Contexts can be composed, i.e., if $Q[]$ and $Q'[]$ are contexts and Q'' a plan such that $Q[Q'[Q'']]$ is also a plan, then $Q[Q'[]]$ is a context.

Given a context $Q[]$ we define a *user query* $\mathsf{Uq}_{[]}(Q)$ to abstract the properties (of variables) *inside of the context*:

$$
\mathsf{Uq}_{[]}(Q) = \begin{cases} \top & Q = [] \\ \mathsf{Uq}(Q_2) \wedge \mathsf{Uq}_{[]}(Q_1[]) & Q = Q_1[Q_2 \wedge []] \text{ or } Q_1[[] \wedge Q_2] \\ \exists x.\,\mathsf{Uq}_{[]}(Q_1[]) & Q = Q_1[\exists x.[]] \\ \mathsf{Uq}_{[]}(Q_1[]) & Q = Q_1[\{[]\}],\, Q_1[\neg[]],\, Q_1[Q_2 \vee []],\, \text{or } Q_1[[] \vee Q_2] \,. \end{cases}
$$

$\square$

With the help of the contexts, we can now reformulate and extend the rules for manipulating the duplicate elimination operator as follows.

Theorem 5.20   (Duplicate Elimination Removal)   Let Q be a plan. Then

$$
\begin{aligned}
Q[\{R(x_1, \ldots, x_k)\}] &\leftrightarrow Q[R(x_1, \ldots, x_k)] \\
Q[\{Q_1 \wedge Q_2\}] &\leftrightarrow Q[\{Q_1\} \wedge \{Q_2\}] \\
Q[\{\neg Q_1\}] &\leftrightarrow Q[\neg Q_1] \\
Q[\neg\{Q_1\}] &\leftrightarrow Q[\neg Q_1] \\
Q[\{Q_1 \vee Q_2\}] &\leftrightarrow Q[\{Q_1\} \vee \{Q_2\}] \quad \text{if } \Sigma \cup \{\mathsf{Uq}_{[]}(Q[])\} \models Q_1 \wedge Q_2 \to \bot \\
Q[\{\exists x.Q_1\}] &\leftrightarrow Q[\exists x.\{Q_1\}] \quad \text{if} \\
&\quad \Sigma \cup \{\mathsf{Uq}_{[]}(Q[]) \wedge \mathsf{Uq}(Q_1)[y_1/x] \wedge \mathsf{Uq}(Q_1)[y_2/x]\} \models y_1 \approx y_2 \,,
\end{aligned}
$$

where y_1 and y_2 are fresh variable names not occurring in Q, Q_1, and Q_2. In addition, it is always the case that $Q[\{Q_1[\{Q_2\}]\}] \leftrightarrow Q[\{Q_1[Q_2]\}]$. $\square$

Similar approach can be used to generalize *cut insertion* (see Exercise 5.10).

5.4   INTERPOLATION VS. CHASE

We have already shown that for certain physical designs, the chase-based technique is not sufficient (see Example 5.14).

Now we argue that chase can be *simulated* by interpolation. For example, a single chase step for $\varphi_1, \ldots, \varphi_m$ with $\forall \mathbf{x}.(\psi_1 \wedge \ldots \wedge \psi_k) \rightarrow (\exists \mathbf{y}.\phi_1 \wedge \ldots \wedge \phi_n)$ in $\mathsf{chase}_\Sigma(Q)$ can be simulated by the following proof fragment:

$$
\cfrac{
\cfrac{
\Gamma, \neg\theta(\psi_1), \varphi_1, \ldots, \varphi_m \vdash \Delta \; \ldots \\
\Gamma, \neg\theta(\psi_k), \varphi_1, \ldots, \varphi_m \vdash \Delta
}{
\Gamma, \neg\theta(\psi_1) \vee \ldots \vee \neg\theta(\psi_k), \varphi_1, \ldots, \varphi_m \vdash \Delta
}
\qquad
\cfrac{
\cfrac{
\vdots
}{
\Gamma, \theta(\phi_1)[\mathbf{z}/\mathbf{y}], \ldots, \theta(\phi_n)[\mathbf{z}/\mathbf{y}], \\ \varphi_1, \ldots, \varphi_m \vdash \Delta
}
}{
\Gamma, \theta(\exists \mathbf{y}.\phi_1 \wedge \ldots \wedge \phi_n), \varphi_1, \ldots, \varphi_m \vdash \Delta
}
}{
\cfrac{
\Gamma, \theta(\neg\psi_1 \vee \ldots \vee \neg\psi_k) \vee \theta(\exists \mathbf{y}.\phi_1 \wedge \ldots \wedge \phi_n), \varphi_1, \ldots, \varphi_m \vdash \Delta
}{
\Gamma, \forall \mathbf{x}.(\neg\psi_1 \vee \ldots \vee \neg\psi_k) \vee (\exists \mathbf{y}.\phi_1 \wedge \ldots \wedge \phi_n), \varphi_1, \ldots, \varphi_m \vdash \Delta
}
} ,
$$

where $\mathbf{x}$ stands for $x_1, \ldots, x_\ell$ (similar for $\mathbf{y}$ and $\mathbf{z}$). Note that in the left part of the proof, the branches for the premises of the dependency, after the proper substitution arising from the universal quantifier inference rule, each immediately end in an axiom. On the right side of the proof, the consequents of the dependency are added to the partial chase and then the existential quantifiers are processed but the corresponding inference rule to essentially obtain a conjunction of atoms. Note that additional proof steps may be needed to handle equalities in the consequent. The remainder of the simulation is similar; see Exercise 5.9.

5.5   SUMMARY

Techniques for automatic generation of plans that implement user queries—query compilation—are deeply rooted in theorem proving techniques, such as the *chase* (in the case of conjunctive queries and dependencies) or the *tableaux* proof system and interpolation (in the case of full first-order logic). An interesting observation at this point is that there is an inherent connection between alternative proofs in the underlying proof systems and alternative plans for a user query.

In practice, the proof systems and the proof search strategies used to compile queries must be enhanced with additional extra-logical considerations, such as satisfaction of binding patterns, considerations of inherent ordering of data and the influence of plans on such orderings, and the estimated cost of alternative query plans. These features distinguish the actual techniques used for query compilation from the off the shelf theorem proving approaches that mainly focus on heuristics that attempt to find an arbitrary proof as fast s possible.

While the proof techniques account for the bulk of the compilation process, they are accompanied by *post-processing* of query plans that is needed to account for subtle differences between the pure first-order semantics of queries and the iterative nature of query plans, such as dealing with duplicates produced by query plans, while retaining reasonable prospects of efficiency.

5.6   BIBLIOGRAPHIC NOTES

The issue of translating user queries to executable and efficient query plans—query compilation—has been the focus of research since the introduction of the relational model by Codd [1970]. The standard approaches, including many commercial RDBMS, assume that for each relation in the logical design, there is a *base file* and possibly several associated *search indices*; in this setting, query compilation typically reduces to cost-based optimization problem [Chaudhuri, 1998, Ioannidis, 1996]. However, in many cases, including use of materialized views, integration of information from multiple sources, and advanced physical designs such as those introduced in Chapter 4, such an assumption is no longer valid. To address this issue, approaches to reformulating user queries in terms of (materialized) views were developed [Levy et al., 1995]. Subsequently, query compilation under constraints formulated in the form of dependencies based on the *chase* [Aho et al., 1979, Maier et al., 1979] was developed by Deutsch et al. [1999]. Handling of duplicates and the associated duplicate elimination operators (needed for more fine-grained appreciation of query plans) was developed by Khizder et al. [2000]. In the same vein, the use of the *cut* operators based on functional constraints was proposed by Mendelzon and Wood [1991]. Nash et al. [2010] have shown shortcomings of chase-based query compilation approaches. For first-order queries and constraints, the work of Beth [1953] on implicit definability yields a complete criterion for existence of query plan and *Craig interpolation* [Craig, 1957] combined with an appropriate proof system, such as the *sequent calculus* [Gentzen, 1935], provides means for synthesis of query plans. The interpolation-based techniques are complete if arbitrary interpretations are considered; if only finite interpretations are allowed, the methods remain sound, albeit incomplete [Ebbinghaus and Flum, 1999].

5.7   EXERCISES WITH TOPICS FOR DISCUSSION

Exercise 5.1   Extend Example 5.6 to arbitrary conjunctions: show that the execution only depends on the *order* of conjuncts, but not on how parentheses are put in the expression.

Exercise 5.2   Show that conjunctive queries have normal form. How is this related to comparisons and assignments that appear in conjunctive plans?

Exercise 5.3   Show a procedure that, given an output of the chase rewriting procedure, inserts comparisons to convert it to a plan. Do you need to consider assignments?

Exercise 5.4   Formulate the constraints in Example 4.7 as dependencies and show how the extended chase derives the plan in Example 5.13.

Exercise 5.5   Revise the interpolation rules in Figure 5.2 to accommodate binding patterns.

Exercise 5.6   Show a derivation, using the tools developed in Example 5.18, that synthesizes the plan $aa(x)$ for the user query $a(x) \vee a(x)$. Using a similar idea, create a design that accommodates the distributive law, i.e., finds the plan $aa(x) \wedge (bb(x) \vee \wedge cc(x))$ for the user query

$$(a(x) \wedge b(x)) \vee (a(x) \wedge c(x)).$$

Exercise 5.7   Design a procedure that, given a physical design, produces another physical design that supports the same user queries but in which it is always possible to factor common subexpressions from interpolants (i.e., generalize Exercise 5.6).

Exercise 5.8   Careful reading of the interpolation rules reveals that the given user query structure may impose an order on joins that can appear in the interpolants (note that there is no *commutativity of conjunctions* rule explicitly present). Show an example where this can actually happen. Then show how generating alternative *join ordering* can be accommodated using the technique in Example 5.18.

Exercise 5.9   Complete the proof that simulates the rest of the chase. Hint: use the technique introduced in Example 5.18 to handle the *selection of plan atoms* in the third step of the chase.

Exercise 5.10   Use the notion of a context (Definition 5.19) to extend the result of Theorem 5.11 to first-order plans.

CHAPTER 6

Updating Data

We now investigate how the *plan synthesis* approaches can be applied to the problem of database updates. The general framework is a follows.

1. The user issues a request to add (insert) and remove (delete) sets of tuples to/from an instance of a logical relation.

2. This request is then translated to possibly multiple requests that modify *all* the access paths in the associated physical design.

Since modification requests must be *consistency-preserving* (i.e., the result of the modification must satisfy all integrity constraints in the schema) and this may require modifying the instances of *several* logical relations simultaneously, we henceforth assume that a *modification request* is specified by a set of such requests (perhaps trivially empty), one for each symbol in the logical design.

We mainly consider OPTION 1-style logical design for most of this chapter since it is inherently *value-based*. OPTION 3 causes slight problems for updates because the user is required to supply *object ids* to specify the updates—this is slightly inconvenient despite the fact that any unique values would work for this purpose using the development described in this chapter.

6.1 USER VS. PHYSICAL UPDATES

Given a physical design $\langle S_L \cup S_P, \Sigma \rangle$ and access paths $S_A \subseteq S_P$, we define, for each non-logical (relational) symbol R in $S_L \cup S_P$, the following symbols:

- R^o to represent the *old* instance of R (i.e., before the update);

- R^n to represent the *new* instance of R (i.e., after the update);

- R^+ to represent the *added tuples* (i.e., $R^n - R^o$); and

- R^- to represent the *removed tuples* (i.e., $R^o - R^n$).

We call the symbols R^+ and R^- *delta relations* (*deltas* for short). Note that an instance $\mathcal{I}$ of this new vocabulary captures both the instance before and the instance after the modification request. In this setting, a *user modification request* is specified as a set of pairs of instances

$$\{((R^+)^{\mathcal{I}}, (R^-)^{\mathcal{I}}) \mid R \in S_L\} .$$

Since the goal of the update is to determine the *new* instances of all *access paths* (or the added and removed tuples for each such access path) given the changes to *all* logical (user-defined) relations, we consider the following derived physical design.

Logical Signature: the logical symbols (including the symbols that logically describe the changes to all access paths) consist of the logical symbols for both the *old* and the *new* instances of the data, S_L^o and S_L^n, respectively, the symbols for the access paths of the *new* instance, $\{R^n/k \mid R/k/i \in S_A\}$, and the symbols $S_L^{\pm} = \{R^+/k, R^-/k \mid R/k/i \in S_A\}$.

Physical Signature and Access Paths: the access paths in the derived physical design consist of the access paths $S_A^o = \{R^o/k/i \mid R/k/i \in S_A\}$ for accessing the *old* instance of the data using the original design, and the user supplied data that specify the modification request, $S_A^{\pm} = \{R^+/k/0, R^-/k/0 \mid R/k \in S_L\}$.

Constraints: the constraints consist of the original constraints (over the *old* symbols), Σ^o, the same constraints over the *new* symbols, Σ^n, and constraints that define the sets of added/removed tuples

$$\Sigma^{\pm} = \{ \forall x_1, \ldots, x_k . R^+(x_1, \ldots, x_k) \equiv R^n(x_1, \ldots, x_k) \wedge \neg R^o(x_1, \ldots, x_k),$$
$$\forall x_1, \ldots, x_k . R^-(x_1, \ldots, x_k) \equiv R^o(x_1, \ldots, x_k) \wedge \neg R^n(x_1, \ldots, x_k)$$
$$\mid R/k \in S_L \cup S_P \},$$

where Σ^o and Σ^n are copies of the set of formulae Σ in which each symbol R was replaced by R^o and R^n, respectively.

The new physical design, which we call the *update design* (associated with an given physical design), then consists of logical signature $S_L^o \cup S_L^n \cup S_L^{\pm}$, the access paths $S_A^o \cup S_A^{\pm}$, and the constraints $\Sigma^o \cup \Sigma^n \cup \Sigma^{\pm}$.

This setting effectively converts the issue of *how to update the data* (in the original design) to *how to find a query plan* that computes the tuples that need to be inserted into or deleted from every individual access path (in the update design). Note that the actual primitive insertions and deletions must be represented by black boxes similar to primitive access paths (as introduced in Chapter 3).

6.1.1   UPDATES, DEFINABILITY, AND PLANS

Given the above update design, we need a straightforward way to determining whether an user update request can be propagated from the deltas expressed in the terms of the original logical symbols S_L to deltas over the access paths S_A. This, however, is equivalent to determining whether the *new state* R^n (or, equivalently, the deltas R^+ and R^-) for every access path in S_A is definable and whether a plan can be generated for it with respect to the *update design*.

Example 6.1   We illustrate this again on Example 3.2 from Chapter 3 where the integrity constraints are

$$\Sigma = \{ \ \forall x, y, z.(\texttt{employee}(x, y, z) \rightarrow \texttt{emp-array0}(z, x, y)),$$
$$\forall x, y, z.(\texttt{emp-array0}(z, x, y) \rightarrow \texttt{employee}(x, y, z)) \ \},$$

and $S_A = \{$emp-array0/3/0$\}$. Hence, the update design is as follows:

$$\Sigma^u = \{\, \forall x, y, z.(\text{employee}^o(x, y, z) \rightarrow \text{emp-array0}^o(z, x, y)),$$
$$\forall x, y, z.(\text{emp-array0}^o(z, x, y) \rightarrow \text{employee}^o(x, y, z)),$$
$$\forall x, y, z.(\text{employee}^n(x, y, z) \rightarrow \text{emp-array0}^n(z, x, y)),$$
$$\forall x, y, z.(\text{emp-array0}^n(z, x, y) \rightarrow \text{employee}^n(x, y, z)),$$
$$\forall x, y, z.(\text{employee}^+(x, y, z) \equiv \text{employee}^n(x, y, z) \wedge \neg\text{employee}^o(x, y, z)),$$
$$\forall x, y, z.(\text{employee}^-(x, y, z) \equiv \text{employee}^o(x, y, z) \wedge \neg\text{employee}^n(x, y, z)),$$
$$\forall x, y, z.(\text{emp-array0}^+(x, y, z) \equiv \text{emp-array0}^n(x, y, z) \wedge \neg\text{emp-array0}^o(x, y, z)),$$
$$\forall x, y, z.(\text{emp-array0}^-(x, y, z) \equiv \text{emp-array0}^o(x, y, z) \wedge \neg\text{emp-array0}^n(x, y, z))\,\},$$

with $S_A^u = \{$emp-array0^o/3/0, employee$^+$/3/0, employee$^-$/3/0$\}$.   □

Formulating *user queries* that ask about the contents of the deltas for the access paths in the original design and subsequently synthesizing plans for these provides the basic tool for propagating updates from user relations to access paths (in the original design).

Example 6.2   Using the update design in Example 6.1, we can ask, e.g., for the tuples to be inserted into emp-array0 based on user's update request as a user query, emp-array0$^+(x, y, z)$. It is easy to see that for this user query we can find that a plan employee$^+(y, z, x)$ implements this query, e.g., as

$$\text{emp-array0}^+(x, y, z) \equiv (\text{emp-array0}^n(x, y, z) \wedge \neg\text{emp-array0}^o(x, y, z))$$
$$\equiv (\text{employee}^n(y, z, x) \wedge \neg\text{employee}^o(y, z, x)) \equiv \text{employee}^+(y, z, x)$$

logically follows from Σ^u and employee$^+$/3/0 $\in S_A^u$. Hence, this plan computes the tuples that need to be *inserted* to the access path emp-array0.   □

Note that to find the above *update plan* automatically we need to use the interpolation-based technique from Section 5.3 since the constraints contain negations (see Exercise 6.1).

The *update plans* simply generate the appropriate tuples to be inserted into or deleted from a particular access path of the underlying design. Additional primitives are also needed that actually perform the individual insertions and deletions: these must be provided (as additional code) by the DBA; this similar to needing code for the primitive access paths (see Chapter 3).

Example 6.3   Figure 6.1 shows a pseudocode for primitive insertion and deletion (for simplicity it assumes there is always space for a new *employee* in the array).   □

The code for primitive insertions and deletions is then combined with the synthesized update plans, e.g., as follows:

```
if  Q⁺-first                         if  Q⁻-first
    repeat                               repeat
               Q-insert    and                    Q-delete
    until not  Q⁺-next                   until not  Q⁻-next
```

```
function emp-array0-insert              function emp-array0-delete
    n := n + 1                             i := 1
    emp-array0[n].emp-salary := x1          while i <= n do
    emp-array0[n].emp-num := x2               if (emp-array0[i].emp-num = x2)
    emp-array0[n].emp-name := x3                move emp-array0[i+1,n] to
    return                                                  emp-array[i,n-1]
                                                n := n - 1
                                          i := i + 1
                                          return
```

Figure 6.1: Primitive insertion and deletion for the `emp-array0` access path.

where Q is the name of the access path in question. A sequence of code fragments such as above is then generated for every access path. Alternatively, we could use the notion of access path and binding pattern(s) to create an access path that would effectively force the execution of the above code fragment and that would be compiled into the update plan itself (see Exercise 6.2).

6.2   UPDATES AND COMPLEMENTS

The approach from the previous section works only for physical designs that do not need to *invent new values*, such as addresses of records to actually store the data (see Example 4.1). Indeed, when trying to apply the above approach in that setting, we quickly find that none of the new states of the access paths is definable in terms of the update design.

The way to address this problem is to provide additional *access path*s that, conceptually, provide all the possible values that may be needed for the insertion (e.g., an address of *any possible* emp record). Such an access path is commonly called the *complement* (of the set of emp records that are already present in the database instance). For example, (and as a first cut), we could define an access path *empcomp/5/4* that, given an *employee* number, name, salary, and (reference to) a department, produces a reference to (an address of) an appropriate emp record whose fields contain the given four values. This new access path is linked to the rest of the design using constraints, such as:

$$\forall x, y, z, t.\texttt{employee}(x, y, z) \wedge \texttt{works}(x, t) \rightarrow \exists v.\texttt{empcomp}(x, y, z, t, v)$$
$$\forall v.\texttt{empfile}(v) \rightarrow \exists x, y, z, t.\texttt{empcomp}(x, y, z, t, v)$$
$$\forall x, y, z, t, v, w.\texttt{empcomp}(x, y, z, t, w) \wedge \texttt{empcomp}(x, y, z, t, v) \rightarrow v \approx w$$
$$\forall x, y, z, t.\texttt{int}(x) \wedge \texttt{string}(y) \wedge \texttt{int}(z) \wedge \texttt{deptref}(t) \rightarrow \exists v.\texttt{empcomp}(x, y, z, t, v) \,,$$

and so on. The constraints state that the complement empcomp is compatible with all employee records in existence and that any other employee record can be created. There are two issues with this basic idea.

```
function empcomp-first                          function empcomp-next
    if an emp record ⟨x₅, x₁, x₂, x₃, x₄⟩           return false
        exists for some x₅ return true
    x₅ := new emp
    x₅->num    := x₁;    x₅->name := x₂;
    x₅->salary := x₃;    x₅->dept := x₄;
    return true
```

Figure 6.2: Complement for emp records.

1. We need to provide a feasible implementation of the empcomp access path: it isn't feasible to assume we have truly stored every possible tuple somewhere.

2. We need to make certain that the binding patterns associated with the *complements* can be satisfied.

For the first problem, we can (as a first attempt) use the pseudo-code in Figure 6.2. Note that the test for *existence* of an record, in addition to determining if such a record already exists in the current instance of the database, must also ensure such a record has not been already created during the processing of the update plans (but perhaps not yet physically inserted into an appropriate access path). This in general requires the implementation of the complement access path to remember what new records it has created within a transaction; we revisit this issue in Section 6.3.1.

6.2.1   COMPLEMENTS VS. A CYCLIC SCHEMA

The second issue requires a slight adjustment to the basic idea of complement. In particular, consider a situation in which we are trying to add the first department and first employee: to satisfy the binding patterns for the complement access paths defined above, the *address* of the new dept record is needed in order to create the new emp record and vise versa. Hence, we will fail to synthesize an appropriate plan. However, in a way analogous to the physical design for records and fields that allows separate access to the individual fields of a single record using multiple access paths, we can separate the allocation of a record given a key and inserting it into the appropriate access path(s) from filling the fields of the record with the required (remaining) values. Note that it is essential to provide the complement access path with the *key* of the record created so it can check whether such a record *already exists* and return the appropriate address.

Example 6.4 (Complements and Updating emp and dept)   Consider the update design corresponding to Example 4.1 together with the access paths in Figures 6.2 and 6.3. For an update request to *create a new department and add its employees among which is the manager of the new department*, we can now generate the following update plans:

```
function deptcomp-first                         function deptcomp-next
    if an dept record with dept.num = x₁            return false
        exists at address x₂ return true
    x₂ := new dept
    x₂->num := x₁
    return true
```

Figure 6.3: Complement for dept records.

1. for $\texttt{deptfile}^+(x)$:

$$\exists y, z, t.\texttt{department}^+(z, y, t) \wedge \texttt{deptcomp}(z, x) \, ;$$

2. for $\texttt{dept-name}^+(x, y)$:

$$\exists z, t.\texttt{department}^+(z, y, t) \wedge \texttt{deptcomp}(z, x) \, ;$$

3. for $\texttt{empfile}^+(x)$:

$$\exists y, z, t, u, v.\texttt{employee}^+(y, z, t) \wedge \texttt{works}^+(y, u)$$
$$\wedge \texttt{deptcomp}(u, v) \wedge \texttt{empcomp}(y, z, t, v, x);$$

4. for $\texttt{dept-manager}^+(x, y)$:

$$\exists z, t, u. \texttt{department}^+(z, t, u) \wedge \texttt{deptcomp}(z, x)$$
$$\wedge (\exists z, t, v, w.\texttt{employee}^+(u, z, t) \wedge \texttt{works}^+(u, v)$$
$$\wedge \texttt{deptcomp}(v, w) \wedge \texttt{empcomp}(u, z, t, w, y) \,)$$

and the results of these plans are then *reflected* in the instance using the appropriate primitive insertions (see, e.g., Figure 6.4). Note that we have not generated an update plan, e.g., for the dept-num, since the appropriate value is placed in the dept record by the complement access path deptcomp (similarly for the fields of the emp records). □

Note that, although the order of (1–4) is immaterial because of our definition of *complement*s, it is essential that the complement for dept records can be used *without* supplying the reference to that department's manager. This omission is later *repaired* by the plan for dept-manager⁺ that, rather than allocating new record(s), simply initializes a field of an *existing* dept record with the appropriate value: an address of an emp record representing the manager of the department. Also note that (1) and (2) could be *merged* into a single plan and primitive insertion and, unlike for queries, full reification is not always optimal. And finally note that the complement must obtain at least the key as input for this to work (and thus it becomes unnecessary to initialize the key fields later on).

```
function dept-name-insert          function dept-manager-insert
  x₁->name := x₂                     x₁->manager := x₂
  return                             return
```

Figure 6.4: Primitive insertions for the `dept-name` and `dept-manager` access paths.

6.2.2 UPDATE TYPES

The update plans in Example 6.4 only work under the assumption that one of the *new* employees will become the manager of the newly-created department. This requirement (stated informally in the example) can be captured by an additional *integrity constraint* over the deltas, in this case:

$$\forall x, y, z.\texttt{department}^+(x, y, z) \rightarrow \exists t, u.\texttt{employee}^+(z, t, u) \wedge \texttt{works}^+(z, x) \, .$$

Such additional constraints are then added to the update design's Σ^u and affect the existence and shape of update plans (see Exercises 6.3 and 6.4). By using constraints on the deltas, we can stipulate that:

- certain logical symbols must be updated separately from others (by asserting, for that update type, that the other symbol's deltas are empty);

- certain symbols can only be inserted into (by asserting that the negative delta is empty);

- updates of certain symbols must be using single tuple at a time only (by asserting that the delta is a singleton), etc.

In addition, update types that postulate no change to certain user predicates can (and in many practical cases do) imply no changes to some of the associated access paths which, in turn simplifies the overall update plan.

6.3 PROGRESSIVE UPDATES

There is another issue with the solution in Example 6.4: it assumes that the results of all the update plans are computed *before* the *insertion* code is executed (which, in practice, is problematic). For example, consider executing the insertions to `empfile` *prior to* evaluating the `dept-manager`$^+$ delta in the example above. In this case, our assumptions about access paths when synthesizing this update plan would no longer be *valid* since, for example, `empfile` at this point corresponds to the *new* state of the database instead of the old state. Hence, the assumptions about availability of access paths we made initially may no longer hold (see Exercise 6.3).

We can work around this issue by *changing the update design* to reflect the progress of updating the individual access paths.

Example 6.5   Consider executing the update plans (1-3) in Example 6.4. After executing the third step, the *current* emp records accessible using the empfile access path correspond to the *new* state of the employee relation, employee^n. This can be reflected in the update design by modifying the set of available access paths S_A by removing empfile^o (and emp-num^o, emp-name^o, emp-salary^o, and emp-dept^o) and replacing it by empfile^n (and all the access paths for the fields). The last step of the update plan could then be given as follows:

4′. for dept-manager$^+(x, y)$:

$$\exists z, t, u.\, \text{department}^+(z, t, u) \land \text{deptcomp}(z, x) \land \text{empfile}^n(y) \land \text{emp-num}^n(y, u),$$

where empfile^n and emp-num^n refer to the (new states of the) access paths empfile and emp-num, respectively. Note that, in this formulation, any employee can become the manager of the new department. And should we wish to enforce the original restriction, we can simply add the conjunct

$$\exists x, y.\text{employee}^+(u, x, y)$$

to restrict the allowed managers.   □

Care needs to be taken when records with partially instantiated fields are created. For example, after executing steps 1 and 2 in Example 6.4, the manager field of the new emp records has not been assigned a proper value, but these records can in principle be accessed through the access path deptfile. There are several approaches to this issue:

1. we can remove any access path containing partially instantiated records from the update design;

2. we can remove the access paths accessing the potentially uninstantiated fields; or

3. we can instantiate the fields with a default value, such as the NULL value discussed in Section 4.2, and extend the update design to properly account for the possibility of such a value existing.

While the first two approaches can be automatically generated, the third requires a revision of the constraints Σ^u associated with the design; in particular, it may lead to *weakening* of certain foreign key constraints in a similar fashion to Example 4.5 to accommodate the (transient) need for the default NULL value (in our example used for the yet unknown reference to an emp record).

Additional care must be taken when *insertions* are decoupled from *deletions* to the same access path, even when assuming that the deltas are disjoint (i.e., we never insert a tuple we have just deleted and vice versa). Such a decoupling can leave access paths in a state that corresponds neither to the old nor to the new state, such as in cases where all insertions have been performed but deletions are still pending. Similar to the discussion above, we can create (temporary) access paths corresponding to such instances and link them to the rest of the update design using constraints.

Example 6.6   After performing insertions into the access path `empfile` but before performing any deletions, we can access the partially modified set of `emp` records as follows:

- we create an access path $\texttt{empfile}^{o+}/1/1$, and

- we add a constraint $\forall x.\texttt{empfile}^{o+}(x) \equiv (\texttt{empfile}^{o}(x) \lor \texttt{empfile}^{+}(x))$.

This access path will be available up to the point in the sequence of updates where the deletions on `empfile` are executed; then the access path turns into $\texttt{empfile}^{n}$ as discussed above.   □

The case when tuples are being deleted first is analogous.

6.3.1   CONSTANT SPACE COMPLEMENTS

The last issue relates to *optimizing* the behaviour of the complement access paths: as designed so far, these access paths are (operationally) responsible for allocating new records. To prevent multiple physical records being allocated for the same tuple (key), the access path holds a list of records it has already allocated (see Figure 6.3). For small updates, this solution works well since the few record pointers can be easily kept in memory. However, for large updates such as *bulk loading*, we would prefer to dispose of the need to remember whether a record has already been created and simply allocate a new record each time the complement access path is invoked. To be able to use such *simplified* complement access paths, we must ensure the following two conditions are satisfied.

1. The complement access path must be supplied a key of each record to be created *exactly once*. This can be guaranteed, e.g., by requiring this access path to be used only in a top-level nested-loop join and by ensuring that the rest of the plan generating these keys will never produces a duplicate value; this can be ensured using the technique from Section 5.2.6.

2. The complement access path can be used only *once* in all the individual updates. This requires that the new records are *inserted* into some other access path where they can be found later. Here, the use of the progressive update technique is essential.

Example 6.7   (Single Use of Complements)   Let us return to Example 6.4. Under the above restrictions, and assuming the steps below are executed sequentially, we can generate the following update plans:

1. for $\texttt{deptfile}^{+}(x)$:

    $\exists y, z, t.\texttt{department}^{+}(z, y, t) \land \texttt{deptcomp}(z, x)$;

2. for $\texttt{dept-name}^{+}(x, y)$:

    $\exists z, t.\texttt{department}^{+}(z, y, t) \land \texttt{deptfile}(x) \land \texttt{dept-num}(x, z)$;

3. for $\text{empfile}^+(x)$:

$$\exists y, z, t, u, v.\text{employee}^+(y, z, t) \land \text{works}^+(y, u)$$
$$\land\, \text{deptfile}(v) \land \text{dept-num}(v, u) \land \text{empcomp}(y, z, t, v, x);$$

4. for $\text{dept-manager}^+(x, y)$:

$$\exists z, t, u.\text{department}^+(z, t, u) \land \text{deptfile}(x) \land \text{dept-num}(x, z)$$
$$\land\, \text{empfile}(y) \land \text{emp-name}(y, u),$$

and the results of these plans are then *reflected* in the instance by again using the appropriate primitive insertions. Note how, in steps 2, 3, and 4, references to the newly created departments are resolved by scanning the departments using their department number (since the new records are already present in the new instance of `deptfile`) rather than by referencing the complement `deptcomp`. Similar comments hold for the fourth step requiring a reference to a manager record (that must be present in `empfile` after step 3). $\qquad\square$

If we succeed in creating such a single-use update plan, we can then eliminate the need for the complement and simply add the record allocation code to the appropriate primitive insertions as an alternative.

6.4 SUMMARY

The (single-user) update problem over a given logical schema and the way it manifests itself in the underlying physical design can be viewed as an application of the *query compilation* techniques developed in the previous chapter: the goal of *update compilation* is to synthesize plans that define the *deltas* (differences between the pre- and post-update instance) for all *access paths* in the physical design. These plans must be expressed in terms of the pre-update instance and the deltas of the user relations that are supplied by the user as the specification of the logical update request.

It is notable that the tools developed in previous sections allow us to model the complete update problem as an instance of the more general query plan synthesis problem simply by developing a logical description of the update—the *update design*—associated naturally with a given physical design. Only the code for the primitive insertions and deletions must to be supplied externally (as in the case of primitive access paths).

The existence of the plans that define the post-update state of the access path also speaks directly to the classical problem of *view update* in relational systems since views can be easily defined by constraints. That problem is equivalent to the existence of the plans that define the deltas, e.g., the existence of such plans when the logical update only adds tuples to the view is the same as the view being *insertable*.

While the query compilation technique provides the basis for executing updates, care needs to be taken in practice to avoid a need for unbounded temporary storage. Indeed, a naive implementation leads to the need for *simultaneous modification* of all access paths involved, which is hardly feasible.

A more practical approach accounts for *staging* the updates of the access paths while minimizing the storage requirements.

6.5   BIBLIOGRAPHIC NOTES

Properties of database updates defined using sequences of insertions and deletions (and often also modifications, called the IDM transactions) have been studied by Karabeg and Vianu [1991] including simplification and axiomatization of such update requests. Issues connected with determining how current instances of access paths need to be modified to accommodate a user update request (expressed in terms of the logical design) properly generalize the notion of *view update* [Furtado and Casanova, 1985] and thus entail many of the difficulties connected with view update, such as whether a the user view update request can be correctly reflected in the underlying database [Dayal and Bernstein, 1982]. Syntactic approaches to determining whether an view update request is allowable have been developed, e.g., by Keller [1985]. An essential component of the approach to updates is the ability to invent, e.g., fresh record addresses (and other parts of the physical design) during the update—without these, most updates would be disallowed. The technique of *view complements* [Bancilhon and Spyratos, 1981, Cosmadakis and Papadimitriou, 1984] is used for this purpose: the complements define additional access paths that provide the necessary additional information, such as addresses of records, that are needed to update the database instance.

6.6   EXERCISES WITH TOPICS FOR DISCUSSION

Exercise 6.1   Revisit Examples 6.1 and 6.2 to see whether the same could be accomplished using the extensions to chase introduced in Section 5.2.8.

Exercise 6.2   Design an additional access path that inserts (deletes) tuples as a side-effect and then modify the *update design* in such a way that this access path is appropriately added to the update plan for the delta tables associated with an access path and this way executing the plan itself affects the necessary insertions and deletions (without the need for additional *primitive insertion/deletion* code as in Figure 6.1. Argue why, in your solution, it never tries to insert (delete) the same tuple more than once.

Exercise 6.3   Consider again Example 6.4, however, this time require that the manager of the new department(s) must be one of the already existing employees. How will the update plans change in this setting?

Exercise 6.4   Create an update design and example of a update type for which a update plan exists only when the constraints of the type are in place (i.e., without the constraints on the deltas the update plan does not exist).

APPENDIX A

First-Order Logic

Starting in Chapter 2, we use *first-order logic* (FOL) as the language in which to write sentences to capture metadata for an application domain and to write sentences to express user queries and query plans over the underlying vocabularies. Our goal in this Appendix is to provide a brief overview to FOL with the objective of introducing enough material for the reader to have a clear idea of basic syntax and to understand the notion of an *interpretation* or *model* and how relationships between sentences and interpretations are commonly expressed in various ways with the use of the symbol "$\models$".

We begin by considering vocabularies. Indeed, recall from Chapter 1 that the first steps in arriving at a logical database design are to settle on a choice of names for relevant kinds of entities and attributes.

A.1 SIGNATURES

In FOL, a vocabulary corresponds to a selection of symbols that are used to refer to predicates and functions. This selection of symbols is called a *signature* and is chosen from a space of all such possibilities called the *non-logical parameters* in FOL.

Definition A.1 (Non-Logical Parameters and Signatures) The *non-logical parameters* in FOL consist of infinite disjoint collections $\{P_1, P_2, \ldots\}$ and $\{f_1, f_2, \ldots\}$ of *predicate symbols* and *function symbols*, respectively. The *arity* of each symbol is a non-negative integer n, denoted $\text{Ar}(P_i)$ or $\text{Ar}(f_i)$. Predicate symbols of arity 0 are also called *propositions*, and function symbols of arity 0 are also called *constants*. We write P/i and f/i to denote, respectively, the predicate P and function f for which $\text{Ar}(P)$ and $\text{Ar}(f)$ is i.

A *signature* S in FOL is a possibly infinite selection of non-logical parameters. We write S^P and S^F to refer to the predicate and function symbols in S, respectively. $\square$

A.2 SYNTAX

Sentences that express constraints on the vocabulary for an application domain, or indeed user queries or query plans over the vocabulary, are captured in FOL by writing *well-formed formulae* over a given signature. A distinguishing feature of FOL is that it allows such formulae to have *quantified subexpressions* that are read "... there exists x such that ...". The "x" in such subexpressions are instances of another variety of symbols in FOL called *variables*.

Definition A.2   (Variables)   The *variables* in FOL, denoted V, consist of a countably infinite collection $\{x_1, x_2, \ldots\}$ of symbols disjoint from the set of non-logical parameters in FOL.   □

In general, we allow arbitrary italicized lowercase identifiers, possibly subscripted, to denote elements of V to improve readability, e.g., "y" or "p_1".

The variables V coupled with a choice of FOL signature S induces a set of formulae according to the following.

Definition A.3   (Terms, Atoms and Well-Formed Formulae)   Let S denote an FOL signature. The following grammars define the *terms*, *atoms* and *well formed formulae* induced by S, denoted TERM(S), ATOM(S) and WFF(S), respectively.

- Term ::= x (where $x \in$ V) | $f(\text{Term}_1, \ldots, \text{Term}_n)$ (where $f/n \in \mathsf{S}^\mathsf{F}$)

- Atom ::= $\text{Term}_1 \approx \text{Term}_2$ | $P(\text{Term}_1, \ldots, \text{Term}_n)$ (where $P/n \in \mathsf{S}^\mathsf{P}$)

- ϕ, ψ ::= Atom | $\neg\phi$ | $(\phi \wedge \psi)$ | $\exists x . \phi$ (where $x \in$ V)

Note that we omit mention of S when the signature is clear from context and write more simply, for example, Term. Also note that we use Greek letters ϕ and ψ, possibly subscripted, to refer to elements of WFF.

The *logical parameters* in FOL are the operators $\{\approx, \neg, \wedge, \exists\}$ that are used in defining well-formed forumulae. The operators are referred to as *equality, negation, conjunction* and *existential quantification*, respectively.   □

In FOL, it is convenient and common practice to include the following additional logical parameters as syntactic shorthand:

- (*disjunction*) "$(\phi \vee \psi)$" $\rightsquigarrow$ "$\neg(\neg\phi \wedge \neg\psi)$";

- (*implication*) "$(\phi \rightarrow \psi)$" $\rightsquigarrow$ "$(\neg\phi \vee \psi)$";

- (*equivalence*) "$(\phi \equiv \psi)$" $\rightsquigarrow$ "$((\phi \rightarrow \psi) \wedge (\psi \rightarrow \phi))$"; and

- (*universal quantification*) "$\forall x.\phi$" $\rightsquigarrow$ "$\neg\exists x.\neg\phi$".

It is also convenient and common practice to omit parenthesis in well-formed formulae when intentions are clear, e.g., "$(\phi_1 \wedge \phi_2 \wedge \phi_3)$" instead of "$(\phi_1 \wedge (\phi_2 \wedge \phi_3))$".

Definition A.4   (Free Variables)   Let S denote an FOL signature, and let Term and WFF denote the terms and well-formed formulae induced by S. For any given $t \in$ Term or $\phi \in$ WFF, Fv(t) and

$\mathsf{Fv}(\phi)$ denote the *free variables* of a term and of a well formed formula, respectively, and are inductively defined as follows:

$$\mathsf{Fv}(t) \;=\; \begin{cases} \{x\} & \text{if } t = \text{``}x\text{''}, \text{ and} \\ \bigcup_{1 \le i \le n} \mathsf{Fv}(t_i) & \text{when } t = \text{``}f(t_1, \ldots, t_n)\text{''} \text{ otherwise.} \end{cases}$$

$$\mathsf{Fv}(\phi) \;=\; \begin{cases} \bigcup_{1 \le i \le n} \mathsf{Fv}(t_i) & \text{if } \phi = \text{``}P(t_1, \ldots, t_n)\text{''}, \\ \mathsf{Fv}(t_1) \cup \mathsf{Fv}(t_2) & \text{if } \phi = \text{``}t_1 \approx t_2\text{''}, \\ \mathsf{Fv}(\psi) & \text{if } \phi = \text{``}\neg\, \psi\text{''}, \\ \mathsf{Fv}(\psi_1) \cup \mathsf{Fv}(\psi_2) & \text{if } \phi = \text{``}(\psi_1 \wedge \psi_2)\text{''}, \text{ and} \\ \mathsf{Fv}(\psi) - \{x\} & \text{when } \phi = \text{``}\exists x.\psi\text{''} \text{ otherwise.} \end{cases}$$

A well-formed formula ϕ is *closed* if $\mathsf{Fv}(\phi) = \emptyset$. A closed well-formed formula is also called a *sentence*. $\qquad\square$

Definition A.5 (Substitution) Let $\varphi \in \mathsf{WFF}$ be a formula, x a variable and t a term such that $\mathsf{Fv}(t)$ does not contain variables bound (quantified) in φ. A *substitution of t for x in φ* (written $\varphi[t/x]$) is a WFF obtained from φ by syntactically replacing all free occurrences of x by the term t. $\qquad\square$

Substitutions can be composed yielding simultaneous substitutions, denoted θ, for multiple variables in a formula. In this case, we write $\varphi\theta$ to denote the simultaneous application of all substitutions in θ to the formula φ.

Definition A.6 (Theory) A *theory* over signature S in FOL, written $\Sigma(\mathsf{S})$, is a (possibly infinite) subset of $\mathsf{WFF}(\mathsf{S})$. Again, we omit mention of S when the signature is clear from context. $\qquad\square$

A.3   SEMANTICS

Definition A.7 (Interpretations and Valuations) Let S denote a signature in FOL. An *interpretation* of S, written $\mathcal{I}(\mathsf{S})$, is a pair

$$\mathcal{I}(\mathsf{S}) \;=\; \langle \triangle^{\mathcal{I}(\mathsf{S})}, (\cdot)^{\mathcal{I}(\mathsf{S})} \rangle$$

consisting of a non-empty *domain* of entities $\triangle^{\mathcal{I}(\mathsf{S})}$ and an *interpretation function* $(\cdot)^{\mathcal{I}(\mathsf{S})}$ that maps each predicate symbol $P/n \in \mathsf{S_P}$ to a subset of $(\triangle^{\mathcal{I}(\mathsf{S})})^n$ and each function symbol $f/n \in \mathsf{S_F}$ to a total function from $(\triangle^{\mathcal{I}(\mathsf{S})})^n$ to $\triangle^{\mathcal{I}(\mathsf{S})}$. As usual, we omit mention of S in this notation when the signature is clear from context. Also, we write

$$\langle e_1, \ldots, e_n \rangle$$

to denote an arbitrary element of $(\triangle^{\mathcal{I}(S)})^n$, also called an *n-tuple*.

Given an interpretation $\mathcal{I}$ of signature S, a *valuation* over $\mathcal{I}$, written $\mathcal{V}(\mathcal{I})$ (or as $\mathcal{V}$ when $\mathcal{I}$ is clear from context), is a total function from V to $\triangle^{\mathcal{I}}$. Given $x \in V$ and $e \in \triangle^{\mathcal{I}}$, the valuation $\mathcal{V}[x \mapsto e]$ is defined as follows:

$$\mathcal{V}[x_1 \mapsto e](x_2) = \begin{cases} e & \text{if "}x_1\text{" = "}x_2\text{", and} \\ \mathcal{V}(x_2) & \text{otherwise.} \end{cases}$$

A valuation $\mathcal{V}$ is extended to apply to any $t \in$ Term in the way that satisfies

$$\mathcal{V}(t) = (f)^{\mathcal{I}}(\mathcal{V}(t_1), \ldots, \mathcal{V}(t_n))$$

whenever $t = "f(t_1, \ldots, t_n)"$. $\qquad\qquad\qquad\qquad\qquad\qquad\qquad\qquad\qquad\qquad\qquad\qquad$ □

Definition A.8 (Models, Logical Consequence and Inconsistency)   Let S be a signature in FOL and assume $\phi \in$ WFF(S). An interpretation $\mathcal{I}$ of S and valuation $\mathcal{V}$ over $\mathcal{I}$ is a *model* of ϕ, written

$$\mathcal{I}, \mathcal{V} \models \phi \,,$$

if and only if one of the following conditions apply:

- $\phi = "P(t_1, \ldots, t_n)"$ and $\langle \mathcal{V}(t_1), \ldots, \mathcal{V}(t_n)\rangle \in (P)^{\mathcal{I}}$;

- $\phi = "t_1 \approx t_2"$ and $\mathcal{V}(t_1) = \mathcal{V}(t_2)$;

- $\phi = "\neg\psi"$ and $\mathcal{I}, \mathcal{V} \not\models \psi$;

- $\phi = "(\psi_1 \wedge \psi_2)"$, $\mathcal{I}, \mathcal{V} \models \psi_1$ and $\mathcal{I}, \mathcal{V} \models \psi_2$; or

- $\phi = "\exists x.\psi"$ and $\mathcal{I}, \mathcal{V}[x \mapsto e] \models \psi$ for some $e \in \triangle^{\mathcal{I}}$.

Let Σ be a theory over signature S. Then we say that

1. the pair $\mathcal{I}, \mathcal{V}$ is a *model* of Σ if $\mathcal{I}, \mathcal{V} \models \psi$ for all $\psi \in \Sigma$;

2. Σ is *satisfiable* if it has a model and *unsatisfiable* otherwise;

3. ϕ is a *logical consequence* of Σ, written $\Sigma \models \phi$, if and only if, for any model $\mathcal{I}, \mathcal{V}$ of Σ we have $\mathcal{I}, \mathcal{V} \models \phi$.

$\qquad\qquad\qquad\qquad\qquad\qquad\qquad\qquad\qquad\qquad\qquad\qquad\qquad\qquad\qquad\qquad\qquad\qquad\qquad$ □

Thus, the fundamental problem of reasoning in a given FOL theory $\Sigma(S)$ is the problem of *logical implication*: establishing which $\phi \in$ WFF(S) are logical consequences of $\Sigma(S)$.

The following recall additional consequences of these definitions that are of particular utility for our purposes.

OBSERVATION 1. If a theory Σ is unsatisfiable, then $\Sigma \models \phi$ for all $\phi \in \mathsf{WFF(S)}$. $\square$

OBSERVATION 2 (*deduction theorem*; semantic version). Let ψ be a formula and Σ a set of formulas. Then

$$\Sigma \cup \{\psi\} \models \phi \text{ holds if and only if } \Sigma \models \psi \to \phi.$$

Moreover,

$$\Sigma \models \phi \text{ holds if and only if } \Sigma \cup \{\neg\phi\} \text{ is unsatisfiable.}$$

The later observation (in conjunction with a sound and complete proof system) allows for refutation-style arguments. $\square$

OBSERVATION 3. Let $\mathcal{I}$ and ϕ denote an interpretation and sentence over a given signature, respectively. If there exists a valuation $\mathcal{V}$ over $\mathcal{I}$ for which

$$\mathcal{I}, \mathcal{V} \models \phi \, ,$$

then $\mathcal{I}, \mathcal{V}' \models \phi$ for any valuation $\mathcal{V}'$. Conversely, if ψ is a well-formed formula over the signature for which $\emptyset \models \psi$ then

$$\emptyset \models \forall x_1. \cdots . \forall x_n. \psi \, ,$$

where $\mathsf{Fv}(\psi) = \{x_1, \ldots, x_n\}$. $\square$

A.4   PROOFS AND THE SEQUENT CALCULUS

While the notion of *logical implication* semantically relates theories and formulas that are consequences of such theories, it does not provide a syntactic characterization of the relation. Syntactic approaches to formalizing the idea of logical implication, often termed *derivability* or *provability* (to stress their syntactic nature) are the focus of *proof systems*. The goal of such systems is to establish a syntactic relation between sets of formulas (theories) and other formulas that can be *derived* from such theories. More formally:

Definition A.9   (Derivations and Proof Systems)   Let $\Gamma, \Delta \subseteq \mathsf{WFF}$.

A *sequent*, $\Gamma \vdash \Delta$, asserts that Δ can be derived from assumptions Γ,

A *derivation (proof)* of a sequent is a (proof) tree of sequents such that

1. each sequent in a leaf of the tree is an *axiom*, and

2. each sequent in an internal node of the tree is derived from its children using an *inference rule*;

We say that such a proof tree *derives* (proves) the sequent labeling its root.

□

We write $\Sigma \vdash \varphi$ when $\Sigma \vdash \{\varphi\}$ for $\varphi \in$ WFF and $\Sigma \subseteq$ WFF. Many proof systems have been proposed for FOL, among which the best known is the *Hilbert System*. Most of these systems can be formalized using *sequents*. However, for the purposes of this book we use a *structural* system devised by Gentzen [1935]:

Definition A.10   (The (classical) Sequent Calculus (LK))   Let $\Gamma, \Delta \subseteq$ WFF and $\varphi, \psi \in$ WFF. The *sequent calculus* consists of the following axioms and inference rules:

Axiom(s) (states that every formula can be derived from itself)

$$\varphi \vdash \varphi$$

Inference Rules:

> **The Cut Rule** (allows eliminating intermediate formulas and in turn using intermediate results—commonly called lemmas—to facilitate proofs)
>
> $$\frac{\Gamma \vdash \Delta, \varphi \quad \Gamma, \varphi \vdash \Delta}{\Gamma \vdash \Delta} \ .$$

> **Logical Rules** (provide for simplification of logical connectives in assumptions and conclusions of sequents)
>
> $$\frac{\Gamma, \varphi \vdash \Delta}{\Gamma, \varphi \wedge \psi \vdash \Delta} \qquad \frac{\Gamma, \psi \vdash \Delta}{\Gamma, \varphi \wedge \psi \vdash \Delta} \qquad \frac{\Gamma \vdash \varphi, \Delta \quad \Gamma \vdash \psi, \Delta}{\Gamma \vdash \varphi \wedge \psi, \Delta} \ .$$
>
> A similar set of rules is defined for each logical connective of the underlying logic (cf. Figure 5.2 in Chapter 5).

> **Structural Rules** (needed to weaken—generalize—sequents when needed in a proof)
>
> $$\frac{\Gamma \vdash \Delta}{\Gamma, \varphi \vdash \Delta} \qquad\qquad \frac{\Gamma \vdash \Delta}{\Gamma \vdash \varphi, \Delta} \ .$$

□

Variants of Sequent Calculus based on sequences of formulas (rather than on sets of formulas) require additional structural rules to manipulate the ordering of such formulas (the *exchange rule*) and duplicity (the *contraction rule*).

The structural nature of the sequent calculus lien in the observation that, with the exception of the *Cut Rule*, all the remaining inference rules enjoy the *subformula property*: only formulas that appear in the consequent (perhaps as subformulas of more complex formulas) can appear in an antecedent of a rule.

There are two essential properties of the sequent calculus:

1. the system is sound and complete, i.e., $\Sigma \models \varphi$ if and only if $\Sigma \vdash \varphi$;

2. sequent calculus derivations can be restricted, without loss of generality, to those that only use rules that enjoy the *subformula property*, called *cut-free derivations*.

The first property is a standard requirement for any proof system, the second, established by Gentzen in one of his major accomplishments—the *Hauptsatz*—is essential for our purposes as it enables natural extraction of interpolants from cut-free proofs as defined in Figure 5.2 (note that the axioms and inference rules are, without loss of generality, modified that purpose, in particular how *negation* is handled in axioms and inference rules).

Bibliography

Aho, A. V., Beeri, C., and Ullman, J. D. (1979). The theory of joins in relational databases. *ACM Trans. Database Syst.*, 4:297–314. DOI: 10.1145/320083.320091 Cited on page(s) 83

Avron, A. (2008). Constructibility and decidability versus domain independence and absoluteness. *Theor. Comput. Sci.*, 394(3):144–158. DOI: 10.1016/j.tcs.2007.12.008 Cited on page(s) 38

Baader, F., Calvanese, D., McGuinness, D. L., Nardi, D., and Patel-Schneider, P. F., editors (2007). *The Description Logic Handbook: Theory, Implementation, and Applications (second edition)*. Cambridge University Press. Cited on page(s) 19

Bancilhon, F. and Spyratos, N. (1981). Update semantics of relational views. *ACM Trans. Database Syst.*, 6:557–575. DOI: 10.1145/319628.319634 Cited on page(s) 95

Batory, D. S. and Gotlieb, C. C. (1982). A unifying model of physical databases. *ACM Trans. Database Syst.*, 7(4):509–539. DOI: 10.1145/319758.319760 Cited on page(s) 61

Beeri, C. and Vardi, M. Y. (1984). A proof procedure for data dependencies. *J. ACM*, 31(4):718–741. DOI: 10.1145/1634.1636 Cited on page(s) 19

Beth, E. W. (1953). On Padoa's method in the theory of definition. *Indagationes Mathematicae*, 15:330–339. Cited on page(s) 83

Casanova, M. A., Fagin, R., and Papadimitriou, C. H. (1984). Inclusion dependencies and their interaction with functional dependencies. *J. Comput. Syst. Sci.*, 28(1):29–59. DOI: 10.1016/0022-0000(84)90075-8 Cited on page(s) 19

Chaudhuri, S. (1998). An overview of query optimization in relational systems. In *Proceedings of the Seventeenth ACM SIGACT-SIGMOD-SIGART Symposium on Principles of Database Systems*, pages 34–43. ACM Press. DOI: 10.1145/275487.275492 Cited on page(s) 83

Chaudhuri, S. and Vardi, M. Y. (1993). Optimization of *real* conjunctive queries. In *PODS*, pages 59–70. Cited on page(s) 38

Chen, P. P. (1976). The entity-relationship model - toward a unified view of data. *ACM Trans. Database Syst.*, 1(1):9–36. DOI: 10.1145/320434.320440 Cited on page(s) 19

Coburn, N. and Weddell, G. E. (1993). A logic for rule-based query optimization in graph-based data models. In Ceri, S., Tanaka, K., and Tsur, S., editors, *DOOD*, volume 760 of *Lecture Notes in Computer Science*, pages 120–145. Springer. Cited on page(s) 38

Codd, E. F. (1970). A relational model of data for large shared data banks. *Commun. ACM*, 13:377–387. DOI: 10.1145/362384.362685 Cited on page(s) 5, 19, 82

Codd, E. F. (1971). Further normalization of the data base relational model. *IBM Research Report, San Jose, California*, RJ909. Cited on page(s) 19

Codd, E. F. (1972). Relational completeness of data base sublanguages. *In: R. Rustin (ed.): Database Systems: 65-98, Prentice Hall and IBM Research Report RJ 987, San Jose, California.* Cited on page(s) 38

Cosmadakis, S. S. and Papadimitriou, C. H. (1984). Updates of relational views. *J. ACM*, 31:742–760. DOI: 10.1145/1634.1887 Cited on page(s) 95

Craig, W. (1957). Three uses of the Herbrand-Genzen theorem in relating model theory and proof theory. *Journal of Symbolic Logic*, 22:269–285. DOI: 10.2307/2963594 Cited on page(s) 83

Date, C. J. and Hopewell, P. (1971a). File definition and logical data independence. In *Proceedings of the 1971 ACM SIGFIDET (now SIGMOD) Workshop on Data Description, Access and Control*, pages 117–138. DOI: 10.1145/1734714.1734724 Cited on page(s) 5

Date, C. J. and Hopewell, P. (1971b). Storage structure and physical data independence. In *Proceedings of the 1971 ACM SIGFIDET (now SIGMOD) Workshop on Data Description, Access and Control*, pages 139–168. DOI: 10.1145/1734714.1734725 Cited on page(s) 5

Dayal, U. and Bernstein, P. A. (1982). On the correct translation of update operations on relational views. *ACM Trans. Database Syst.*, 7:381–416. DOI: 10.1145/319732.319740 Cited on page(s) 95

Deutsch, A., Popa, L., and Tannen, V. (1999). Physical data independence, constraints, and optimization with universal plans. In *Proceedings of the 25th International Conference on Very Large Data Bases*, VLDB '99, pages 459–470. Cited on page(s) 83

Ebbinghaus, H.-D. and Flum, J. (1999). *Finite model theory (2nd ed.)*. Perspectives in Mathematical Logic. Springer. Cited on page(s) 83

Furtado, A. L. and Casanova, M. A. (1985). Updating relational views. In *Query Processing in Database Systems*, pages 127–142. Springer. Cited on page(s) 95

Gentzen, G. (1935). Untersuchungen über das logische schließen. I. *Mathematische Zeitschrift*, 39:176–210. 10.1007/BF01201353. DOI: 10.1007/BF01201353 Cited on page(s) 83, 102

Ginsburg, S. and Hull, R. (1983). Order dependency in the relational model. *Theor. Comput. Sci.*, 26:149–195. DOI: 10.1016/0304-3975(83)90084-1 Cited on page(s) 38

Hellerstein, J. M., Naughton, J. F., and Pfeffer, A. (1995). Generalized search trees for database systems. In Dayal, U., Gray, P. M. D., and Nishio, S., editors, *Proceedings of the 21st International Conference on Very Large Data Bases*, pages 562–573. Morgan Kaufmann. Cited on page(s) 61

Ioannidis, Y. E. (1996). Query optimization. *ACM Comput. Surv.*, 28(1):121–123. DOI: 10.1145/234313.234367 Cited on page(s) 83

Karabeg, D. and Vianu, V. (1991). Simplification rules and complete axiomatization for relational update transactions. *ACM Trans. Database Syst.*, 16:439–475. DOI: 10.1145/111197.111208 Cited on page(s) 95

Keller, A. M. (1985). Algorithms for translating view updates to database updates for views involving selections, projections, and joins. In *Proceedings of the fourth ACM SIGACT-SIGMOD symposium on Principles of database systems*, pages 154–163. DOI: 10.1145/325405.325423 Cited on page(s) 95

Khizder, V. L., Toman, D., and Weddell, G. E. (2000). Reasoning about duplicate elimination with description logic. In *Proceedings of the First International Conference on Computational Logic*, pages 1017–1032. Springer-Verlag. Cited on page(s) 83

Kim, W. (1990). *Introduction to Object-Oriented Databases*. MIT Press. Cited on page(s) 19

Levy, A. Y., Mendelzon, A. O., Sagiv, Y., and Srivastava, D. (1995). Answering queries using views. In *Proceedings of the fourteenth ACM SIGACT-SIGMOD-SIGART symposium on Principles of database systems*, pages 95–104. DOI: 10.1145/212433.220198 Cited on page(s) 83

Maier, D., Mendelzon, A. O., and Sagiv, Y. (1979). Testing implications of data dependencies. *ACM Trans. Database Syst.*, 4:455–469. DOI: 10.1145/320107.320115 Cited on page(s) 83

Mendelzon, A. O. and Wood, P. T. (1991). Functional dependencies in horn clause queries. *ACM Trans. Database Syst.*, 16:31–55. DOI: 10.1145/103140.103142 Cited on page(s) 83

Nash, A., Segoufin, L., and Vianu, V. (2010). Views and queries: Determinacy and rewriting. *ACM Trans. Database Syst.*, 35:21:1–21:41. DOI: 10.1145/1806907.1806913 Cited on page(s) 83

OWL 2 Web Ontology Language: New Features and Rational (2009). http://www.w3.org/TR/owl2-new-features. Cited on page(s) 19

Parnas, D. L. (1972). On the criteria to be used in decomposing systems into modules. *Commun. ACM*, 15(12):1053–1058. DOI: 10.1145/361598.361623 Cited on page(s) 6

Reiter, R. (1977). On closed world data bases. In *Logic and Data Bases*, pages 55–76. Cited on page(s) 19

Reiter, R. (1980). Data bases: A logical perspective. In *Workshop on Data Abstraction, Databases and Conceptual Modelling*, pages 174–176. DOI: 10.1145/800227.806913 Cited on page(s) 19

Simmen, D. E., Shekita, E. J., and Malkemus, T. (1996). Fundamental techniques for order opti-mization. In Apers, P. M. G., Bouzeghoub, M., and Gardarin, G., editors, *Advances in Database Technology - EDBT'96, 5th International Conference on Extending Database Technology*, volume 1057 of *Lecture Notes in Computer Science*, pages 625–628. Springer. Cited on page(s) 38

Tsatalos, O. G., Solomon, M. H., and Ioannidis, Y. E. (1996). The gmap: A versatile tool for physical data independence. *VLDB J.*, 5(2):101–118. DOI: 10.1007/s007780050018 Cited on page(s) 61

Tsichritzis, D. C. and Lochovsky, F. H. (1982). *Data Models*. Prentice-Hall. Cited on page(s) 19

Ullman, J. D. (1985). Implementation of logical query languages for databases. *ACM Trans. Database Syst.*, 10(3):289–321. DOI: 10.1145/3979.3980 Cited on page(s) 38

Authors' Biographies

DAVID TOMAN

David Toman is an Associate Professor in the David R. Cheriton School of Computer Science at the University of Waterloo. His research focuses on database theory and systems, query processing under constraints and query compilation, as well as temporal aspects of data management, and logic in Computer Science, in general. Recently, he has been focusing on database schema languages based on Description Logic enriched with various forms of identification constraints. The languages investigated in this line of research are tailored to enabling compilation of queries formulated over a high-level conceptual schema to code that is executed over low-level physical layouts of data, such as records and pointer structures. He has published extensively in his research area including preparing invited contributions to several reference collections, such as the Encyclopedia of Database Systems and the Handbook of Temporal Reasoning in Artificial Intelligence. He earned Bachelor's and Master's degrees from the Masaryk University in Czechoslovakia in 1992 and a PhD from Kansas State University in 1996, all in Computer Science. He has been awarded numerous research grants, including the NATO-NSERC Postdoctoral fellowship and the Ontario Premier's Research Excellence Award.

GRANT WEDDELL

Grant Weddell is an Associate Professor in the David R. Cheriton School of Computer Science at the University of Waterloo. His research interests fall generally in the area of databases, broadly interpreted, with a focus on the fundamental problems that surface when one combines high-level formatted data access, e.g., SQL queries on relational databases, with higher level transaction and client interaction models, e.g., models supporting "begin transaction" and "end transaction", and/or more detailed temporal specifications of client interaction. He has a particular interest in databases with an underlying data source that corresponds to the contents of a main memory, and is particularly motivated by applications that involve embedded software that must support very high throughput or very low response time for data access and update. More recently, he has worked on description logics and ontology languages, query containment, and, more generally, semantic query optimization, constraint theory, including temporal constraints and logics, and algorithms and data structures relating to semantic search and tableau-based reasoning.

Printed in the United States
by Baker & Taylor Publisher Services